OLIVER CROMWELL

OLIVER CROMWELL

Lawrence Kaplan
City College of New York

1986
CHELSEA HOUSE PUBLISHERS
NEW YORK
NEW HAVEN   PHILADELPHIA

SENIOR EDITOR: William P. Hansen
PROJECT EDITOR: John W. Selfridge
ASSOCIATE EDITOR: Marian W. Taylor
EDITORIAL COORDINATOR: Karyn Gullen Browne
EDITORIAL STAFF: Maria Behan
        Susan Friedman
        Pierre Hauser
        Perry Scott King
        Kathleen McDermott
        Howard Ratner
        Alma Rodriguez-Sokol
        Bert Yaeger
ART DIRECTOR: Susan Lusk
LAYOUT: Irene Friedman
ART ASSISTANTS: Noreen Lamb
        Carol McDougall
        Victoria Tomaselli
COVER DESIGN: Robin Petersen
PICTURE RESEARCH: Karen Herman

Frontispiece courtesy of The Bettmann Archive

First Printing

Library of Congress Cataloging in Publication Data

Kaplan, Lawrence. OLIVER CROMWELL.

(World leaders past & present)
Bibliography: p.
Includes index
1. Cromwell, Oliver, 1599–1658—Juvenile
literature.   2. Statesmen—Great Britain—Biography—
Juvenile literature.   3. Generals—Great Britain—
Biography—Juvenile literature.   4. Great Britain. Army—
Biography—Juvenile literature.   5. Great Britain—History—
Puritan Revolution, 1642–1660—Juvenile literature.
[1. Cromwell, Oliver, 1599–1658.   2. Statesmen.
3. Generals.   4. Great Britain—History—Puritan
Revolution, 1642–1660]   I. Title.   II. Series.
DA426.K36   1986   941.06′4′0924 [B] [92]   85-28007

ISBN 0-87754-580-4

Chelsea House Publishers
Harold Steinberg, Chairman and Publisher
Susan Lusk, Vice President
A Division of Chelsea House Educational Communications, Inc.

133 Christopher Street, New York, NY 10014

345 Whitney Avenue, New Haven, CT 06510

5014 West Chester Pike, Edgemont, PA 19028

Contents

ADENAUER
ALEXANDER THE GREAT
MARK ANTONY
KING ARTHUR
KEMAL ATATÜRK
CLEMENT ATTLEE
BEGIN
BEN-GURION
BISMARCK
LEON BLUM
BOLÍVAR
CESARE BORGIA
BRANDT
BREZHNEV
CAESAR
CALVIN
CASTRO
CATHERINE THE GREAT
CHARLEMAGNE
CHIANG KAI-SHEK
CHURCHILL
CLEMENCEAU
CLEOPATRA
CORTÉS
CROMWELL
DANTON
DE GAULLE
DE VALERA
DISRAELI
EISENHOWER
ELEANOR OF AQUITAINE
QUEEN ELIZABETH I
FERDINAND AND ISABELLA

FRANCO
FREDERICK THE GREAT
INDIRA GANDHI
GANDHI
GARIBALDI
GENGHIS KHAN
GLADSTONE
HAMMARSKJÖLD
HENRY VIII
HENRY OF NAVARRE
HINDENBURG
HITLER
HO CHI MINH
KING HUSSEIN
IVAN THE TERRIBLE
ANDREW JACKSON
JEFFERSON
JOAN OF ARC
POPE JOHN XXIII
LYNDON JOHNSON
BENITO JUÁREZ
JFK
KENYATTA
KHOMEINI
KHRUSHCHEV
MARTIN LUTHER KING, JR.
KISSINGER
LENIN
LINCOLN
LLOYD GEORGE
LOUIS XIV
LUTHER
JUDAS MACCABEUS
MAO

MARY, QUEEN OF SCOTS
GOLDA MEIR
METTERNICH
MUSSOLINI
NAPOLEON
NASSER
NEHRU
NERO
NICHOLAS II
NIXON
NKRUMAH
PERICLES
PERÓN
QADDAFI
ROBESPIERRE
ELEANOR ROOSEVELT
FDR
THEODORE ROOSEVELT
SADAT
STALIN
SUN YAT-SEN
TAMERLAINE
THATCHER
TITO
TROTSKY
TRUDEAU
TRUMAN
QUEEN VICTORIA
WASHINGTON
CHAIM WEIZMANN
WOODROW WILSON
XERXES
ZHOU ENLAI

ON LEADERSHIP
Arthur M. Schlesinger, jr.

LEADERSHIP, it may be said, is really what makes the world go round. Love no doubt smooths the passage; but love is a private transaction between consenting adults. Leadership is a public transaction with history. The idea of leadership affirms the capacity of individuals to move, inspire and mobilize masses of people so that they act together in pursuit of an end. Sometimes leadership serves good purposes, sometimes bad; but whether the end is benign or evil, great leaders are those men and women who leave their personal stamp on history.

Now, the very concept of leadership implies the proposition that individuals can make a difference. This proposition has never been universally accepted. From classical times to the present day, eminent thinkers have regarded individuals as no more than the agents and pawns of larger forces, whether the gods and goddesses of the ancient world or, in the modern era, race, class, nation, the dialectic, the will of the people, the spirit of the times, history itself. Against such forces, the individual dwindles into insignificance.

So contends the thesis of historical determinism. Tolstoy's great novel *War and Peace* offers a famous statement of the case. Why, Tolstoy asked, did millions of men in the Napoleonic wars, denying their human feelings and their common sense, move back and forth across Europe slaughtering their fellows? "The war," Tolstoy answered, "was bound to happen simply because it was bound to happen." All prior history predetermined it. As for leaders, they, Tolstoy said, "are but the labels that serve to give a name to an end and, like labels, they have the least possible connection with the event." The greater the leader, "the more conspicuous the inevitability and the predestination of every act he commits." The leader, said Tolstoy, is "the slave of history."

Determinism takes many forms. Marxism is the determinism of class, Nazism the determinism of race. But the idea of men and women as the slaves of history runs athwart the deepest human instincts. Rigid determinism abolishes the idea of human freedom—the assumption of free choice that underlies every move we make, every word we speak, every thought we think. It abolishes the idea of human responsibility, since it is manifestly unfair to reward or punish people for actions that are by definition beyond their control. No one can live consistently by any deterministic creed. The Marxist states prove this themselves by their extreme susceptibility to the cult of leadership.

More than that, history refutes the idea that individuals make no difference. In December 1931 a British politician crossing Park Avenue in New York City between 76th and 77th Streets around ten-thirty at night looked in the wrong direction and was knocked down by an automobile—a moment, he later recalled, of a man aghast, a world aglare: "I do not understand why I was not broken like an eggshell or squashed like a gooseberry." Fourteen months later an American politician, sitting in an open car in Miami, Florida, was fired on by an assassin; the man beside him was hit. Those who believe that individuals make no difference to history might well ponder whether the next two decades would have been the same had Mario Contasini's car killed Winston Churchill in 1931 and Giuseppe Zangara's bullet killed Franklin Roosevelt in 1933. Suppose, in addition, that Adolf Hitler had been killed in the street fighting during the Munich *Putsch* of 1923 and that Lenin had died of typhus during the First World War. What would the 20th century be like now?

For better or for worse, individuals do make a difference. "The notion that a people can run itself and its affairs anonymously," wrote the philosopher William James, "is now well known to be the silliest of absurdities. Mankind does nothing save through initiatives on the part of inventors, great or small, and imitation by the rest of us—these are the sole factors in human progress. Individuals of genius show the way, and set the patterns, which common people then adopt and follow."

Leadership, James suggests, means leadership in thought as well as in action. In the long run, leaders in thought may well make the greater difference to the world. But, as Woodrow Wilson once said, "Those only are leaders of men, in the general eye, who lead in action. . . . It is at their hands that new thought gets its translation into the crude language of deeds." Leaders in thought often invent in solitude and obscurity, leaving to later generations the tasks of imitation. Leaders in action—the leaders portrayed in this series— have to be effective in their own time.

And they cannot be effective by themselves. They must act in response to the rhythms of their age. Their genius must be adapted, in a phrase of William James's, "to the receptivities of the moment." Leaders are useless without followers. "There goes the mob," said the French politician hearing a clamor in the streets. "I am their leader. I must follow them." Great leaders turn the inchoate emotions of the mob to purposes of their own. They seize on the opportunities of their time, the hopes, fears, frustrations, crises, potentialities.

8

They succeed when events have prepared the way for them, when the community is waiting to be aroused, when they can provide the clarifying and organizing ideas. Leadership ignites the circuit between the individual and the mass and thereby alters history.

It may alter history for better or for worse. Leaders have been responsible for the most extravagant follies and most monstrous crimes that have beset suffering humanity. They have also been vital in such gains as humanity has made in individual freedom, religious and racial tolerance, social justice and respect for human rights.

There is no sure way to tell in advance who is going to lead for good and who for evil. But a glance at the gallery of men and women in *World Leaders—Past and Present* suggests some useful tests.

One test is this: do leaders lead by force or by persuasion? By command or by consent? Through most of history leadership was exercised by the divine right of authority. The duty of followers was to defer and to obey. "Theirs not to reason why,/ Theirs but to do and die." On occasion, as with the so-called "enlightened despots" of the 18th century in Europe, absolutist leadership was animated by humane purposes. More often, absolutism nourished the passion for domination, land, gold and conquest and resulted in tyranny.

The great revolution of modern times has been the revolution of equality. The idea that all people should be equal in their legal condition has undermined the old structures of authority, hierarchy and deference. The revolution of equality has had two contrary effects on the nature of leadership. For equality, as Alexis de Tocqueville pointed out in his great study *Democracy in America*, might mean equality in servitude as well as equality in freedom.

"I know of only two methods of establishing equality in the political world," Tocqueville wrote. "Rights must be given to every citizen, or none at all to anyone . . . save one, who is the master of all." There was no middle ground "between the sovereignty of all and the absolute power of one man." In his astonishing prediction of 20th-century totalitarian dictatorship, Tocqueville explained how the revolution of equality could lead to the "*Führerprinzip*" and more terrible absolutism than the world had ever known.

But when rights are given to every citizen and the sovereignty of all is established, the problem of leadership takes a new form, becomes more exacting than ever before. It is easy to issue commands and enforce them by the rope and the stake, the concentration camp and the *gulag.* It is much harder to use argument and achievement to overcome opposition and win consent. The Founding Fathers of the United States understood the difficulty. They believed that history had given them the opportunity to decide, as

Alexander Hamilton wrote in the first Federalist Paper, whether men are indeed capable of basing government on "reflection and choice, or whether they are forever destined to depend . . . on accident and force."

Government by reflection and choice called for a new style of leadership and a new quality of followership. It required leaders to be responsive to popular concerns, and it required followers to be active and informed participants in the process. Democracy does not eliminate emotion from politics; sometimes it fosters demagoguery; but it is confident that, as the greatest of democratic leaders put it, you cannot fool all of the people all of the time. It measures leadership by results and retires those who overreach or falter or fail.

It is true that in the long run despots are measured by results too. But they can postpone the day of judgment, sometimes indefinitely, and in the meantime they can do infinite harm. It is also true that democracy is no guarantee of virtue and intelligence in government, for the voice of the people is not necessarily the voice of God. But democracy, by assuring the rights of opposition, offers built-in resistance to the evils inherent in absolutism. As the theologian Reinhold Niebuhr summed it up, "Man's capacity for justice makes democracy possible, but man's inclination to injustice makes democracy necessary."

A second test for leadership is the end for which power is sought. When leaders have as their goal the supremacy of a master race or the promotion of totalitarian revolution or the acquisition and exploitation of colonies or the protection of greed and privilege or the preservation of personal power, it is likely that their leadership will do little to advance the cause of humanity. When their goal is the abolition of slavery, the liberation of women, the enlargement of opportunity for the poor and powerless, the extension of equal rights to racial minorities, the defense of the freedoms of expression and opposition, it is likely that their leadership will increase the sum of human liberty and welfare.

Leaders have done great harm to the world. They have also conferred great benefits. You will find both sorts in this series. Even "good" leaders must be regarded with a certain wariness. Leaders are not demigods; they put on their trousers one leg after another just like ordinary mortals. No leader is infallible, and every leader needs to be reminded of this at regular intervals. Irreverence irritates leaders but is their salvation. Unquestioning submission corrupts leaders and demeans followers. Making a cult of a leader is always a mistake. Fortunately hero worship generates its own antidote. "Every hero," said Emerson, "becomes a bore at last."

The signal benefit the great leaders confer is to embolden the rest of us to live according to our own best selves, to be active, insistent, and resolute in affirming our own sense of things. For great leaders attest to the reality of human freedom against the supposed inevitabilities of history. And they attest to the wisdom and power that may lie within the most unlikely of us, which is why Abraham Lincoln remains the supreme example of great leadership. A great leader, said Emerson, exhibits new possibilities to all humanity. "We feed on genius. . . . Great men exist that there may be greater men."

Great leaders, in short, justify themselves by emancipating and empowering their followers. So humanity struggles to master its destiny, remembering with Alexis de Tocqueville: "It is true that around every man a fatal circle is traced beyond which he cannot pass; but within the wide verge of that circle he is powerful and free; as it is with man, so with communities."

—*New York*

Cancellarij sedes

1

Early Years

England flourished during the long and glorious reign of Queen Elizabeth I. It was a golden age, when explorers such as Sir Francis Drake made daring journeys to the New World, returning with ships brimming with riches and exciting tales of distant shores. The religious foundations of the Middle Ages crumbled, giving way to the Reformation, while in science the sun, rather than the earth, was being called the center of the planetary system. The Elizabethan period was marked by a burst of great literary talent; the plays of William Shakespeare, Christopher Marlowe, and Ben Jonson were performed on stage, and the poetry of Edmund Spenser was published. In the political sphere, the English navy gallantly defeated the Spanish Armada in 1588, preserving England's independence.

On April 25, 1599, in Huntingdon, England, four years before the reign of "Good Queen Bess" came to an end, Oliver Cromwell was born. His family had long been active in political affairs, and Cromwell continued that tradition when he rose to fame and power. One of his most famous relatives was Thomas Cromwell, chief minister to 16th-century Tudor monarch Henry VIII. Thomas was executed

THE BETTMANN ARCHIVE

Young Oliver Cromwell received his initial exposure to Puritanism and its adherents at his first school, which was run by a Puritan minister named Thomas Beard.

Elizabeth I (1533–1603), queen of England, addresses the House of Commons. The queen's insistence that Parliament be primarily an advisory body with no real legislative control alienated its members and ultimately led to the confrontations between Crown and Parliament that brought Oliver Cromwell (1599–1658) to power in the mid-17th century.

by the temperamental king in 1540, but not before a number of his relatives were able to amass a considerable amount of land and wealth.

Even though Oliver Cromwell's immediate family achieved high status as members of the gentry (that group of landowners one step down the social ladder from the nobility) they were decidedly poorer than their relatives. Because Oliver's father, Robert, was a second son, he inherited only a small portion of the family estate. Most of it went instead to his older brother who is said to have squandered the inheritance throwing lavish parties for members of royalty, including King James I.

Oliver Cromwell grew to be an energetic and robust young man. He was not especially tall (about five feet six), not particularly handsome, and he paid little attention to his clothing. Never much concerned with his appearance, it did not seem to bother him when critics would later comment on his manner of dress and poke fun at his large nose. When an artist attempted to paint a flattering portrait of him, Cromwell told him, "Paint my picture truly like me . . . pimples, warts, and everything."

As a teenager, Cromwell was educated at the free school of Huntingdon, a one-classroom school, filled with children of all ages, and run by an austere Puritan named Dr. Thomas Beard. Cromwell, however, was often truant for months, being more interested in sports and fraternizing than in Puritanical studies. At a time when mastery of Latin was considered essential for a complete education, the young Cromwell showed little interest in the subject. He did, however, have an aptitude for mathematics, and he also enjoyed reading history books.

When he was 17, Oliver was sent to Puritan-oriented Sidney Sussex College at Cambridge University to receive "an education considered proper for a gentleman," but he had to drop out after only one year when his father died suddenly on June 24, 1617. Although legally a minor, 18-year-old Cromwell was now the only male in the family (there were six daughters) and was therefore expected to help run the family estate. He soon set off for London to study law at one of the Inns of Court, not because he intended to become a lawyer, but because knowledge of legal matters was considered essential at that time for managing landed property. Perhaps his having to assume at an early age some of the responsibility of managing the family estate gave him the ability to handle the positions of command he would fill throughout his adult life.

While in London, Oliver met his future wife, Elizabeth Bourchier, the daughter of a wealthy city merchant. Marriages that linked urban wealth with the status of land ownership were common at that time, and Cromwell received a considerable dowry when the two married on August 22, 1620. The marriage proved to be a loving one as well as a practical one. In later years, Cromwell, frequently separated from his wife during military campaigns, would write affectionate letters to her. One such letter began: "My dearest, I could not satisfy to omit this post, although I have not much to write; yet indeed I love to write to my dear, who is very much in my heart." It was a fruitful marriage as well; they had eight children, four boys and four girls.

Throughout his life Oliver impressed people with his enormous energy. The energy, however, sometimes worked against him. For instance, important policy decisions required that he sit and contemplate alternatives; he would agonize endlessly, finding it difficult to channel his energy to the task. Once a policy was decided, however, he would move without hesitation, rarely suffering from doubts or second thoughts.

British poet John Milton, who knew Cromwell intimately, attempted to explain Cromwell's rise to fame: "He first acquired government of himself, and over himself acquired the most signal victories; so that on the first day he took the field against the external enemy he was a veteran in arms." The winning of what Milton called Cromwell's "signal victories" was Cromwell's mastery of himself, his own restless impulses. The hard won battles within seemed to prepare Cromwell for those in the field.

Cromwell's means to self-mastery was religion. By the time the English Civil War began in 1642, Cromwell had become a devout Puritan, and this com-

According to contemporary accounts, Oliver's mother, Elizabeth Steward Cromwell, possessed a much stronger personality than her husband, and played by far the greater part in young Oliver's upbringing.

The religious "Settlement" negotiated in 1559 between Elizabeth I — portrayed here in a 1596 engraving — and Parliament accorded the monarch supreme authority in ecclesiastical matters. This relationship of church and state displeased many Puritans.

mitment to Puritanism proved to be the most important motivating force in his life.

On the personal level, Puritanism entailed an experience of conversion. This experience, coming after a spiritual struggle, separated the Puritans from the rest of the population. It established them as a privileged elite who would attain heaven after death if certain duties and obligations, chief among them being a continual war against earthly sin, were fulfilled.

During the years after he married and started to have children, Oliver underwent a religious conversion experience. He had been suffering through a period of illness and depression that had no apparent medical basis. Doctors and others who knew Cromwell began to see him as somewhat of a hypochondriac. But in retrospect it seems that he was in fact going through a difficult period of decision, a mental crisis which produced physical symptoms.

Ultimately Cromwell came out of this stage with new vigor and strength, convinced that God had summoned him to be a member of the elect. "He giveth me to see light in His light. One beam in a dark place hath exceeding much refreshment in it. Blessed be His Name for shining upon so dark a heart as mine!" Certain of his own salvation, Cromwell felt a tremendous sense of relief, but at the same time, felt the weighty responsibility of being a "chosen vessel" of the Lord. He would now dedicate his life to serving God.

As a Puritan, Oliver stood in opposition to the Stuart kings. James I, Elizabeth's successor, had disappointed the Puritans. Because James was raised a Presbyterian, (a Protestant sect similar to Puritanism), they had expected him to sympathize with their dissension from the established Church of England. Instead, the king persecuted the Puritans, and threatened to "harry them out of the land" if they refused to conform to the Anglican church.

When Charles I succeeded his father in 1625, he and Archbishop William Laud, the head of the Church of England, not only moved the country away from strict Protestantism, but, like their predecessors, actively persecuted the Puritans. They

> *A devotee of law, Cromwell was forced to be often lawless; a civilian to the core, he had to maintain himself by the sword; with a passion to construct, his task was chiefly to destroy; the most scrupulous of men, he had to ride roughshod over his own scruples and those of others; the most English of our greater figures, he spent his life in opposition to the majority of Englishmen; a realist, he was condemned to build that which could not last.*
> —JOHN BUCHAN
> British historian

Oliver's father, Robert Cromwell (d. 1617) held land that had once belonged to the Roman Catholic church. His hostility toward Catholicism undoubtedly influenced his son.

THE BETTMANN ARCHIVE

even emphasized more traditionally Catholic ceremonies, complete with choirs, organs, and special clothes for priests. The Puritans strongly believed that such materialistic rituals obstructed the true purpose of worship, which they believed to be the kindling of human understanding and not the mere stirring of the emotions. Moreover, Charles married Princess Henrietta Maria of France, a Catholic, and promised her father King Louis XIII that he would assist him in the suppression of the chief Huguenot (French Protestant) stronghold of La Rochelle. He also agreed to allow Catholics to worship in England. It was during this period that many Puritans left England to settle in North America, mainly in New England, and for a time, Cromwell considered emigrating to Massachusetts.

Religious freedom was not the only right denied to the English under Charles I. The king intended to rule the country absolutely, with no limits to his power, just as the monarchs of France were doing on the continent. He saw it as his "royal prerogative" to command the military and tax the country without restraint. The main resistance to this growing royal tyranny came from England's House of Lords (noble and ecclesiastical advisers to the king) and House of Commons (knights and burgesses) — together forming the legislative assembly known as Parliament.

Cromwell attended his first Parliament in June 1628 as a representative to the House of Commons from Huntingdon. This session of Parliament turned out to be one of the most important ever. In that year Parliament enacted one of the great milestones of history, the Petition of Right. The petition was drawn up in order to take away some of the arbitrary powers Charles assumed through "royal prerogative." It called for him to agree never to raise taxes, or demand forced loans without Parliament's consent, and never imprison any of his subjects without publicly stating the cause and then providing for a fair trial — concessions that represented basic freedoms for the citizens of England. Charles agreed to the petition because he needed his subjects' consent to obtain more money, but before

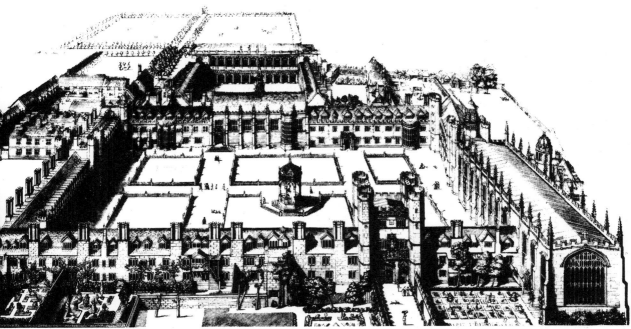

THE BETTMANN ARCHIVE

A 17th-century engraving shows Trinity College, one of the more than 25 colleges that comprise England's Cambridge University. From 1616 to 1617, Cromwell — much to the dismay of his parents, who had expected him to concentrate on civil law and the humanities — devoted himself to studying mathematics at Cambridge's Sidney Sussex College.

long he was once again collecting taxes without authorization.

In 1629 complaints against the king mounted, especially with regard to his religious policies. For the first time, Cromwell took part in the debate in the House of Commons. He criticized the spread of Roman Catholic (papist) practices throughout the land and told the committee how his old friend and teacher Thomas Beard was punished for having called attention to a clergyman who was preaching Catholic doctrines. But before any new charges could be put into law, Charles put an end to this session of Parliament.

Certain members of the House of Commons, including Cromwell, defied the order for adjournment. They passed resolutions condemning all those arbitrary changes in England recently instituted by the king. But these resolutions accomplished little. Charles I now decided to rule England on his own, without any help from Parliament.

For the next 11 years the king ran the country

English philosopher Thomas Hobbes (1588—1679), whose ideas influenced many Puritans, including Cromwell. Hobbes's assertion that a sovereign's power derived from his subjects undermined the monarchists' contention that a king's authority could not be questioned because he ruled by divine right.

himself, pausing only to consult his personal advisers. To pay government expenses new arbitrary taxes and fines were collected by royal agents. One of the most lucrative taxes imposed was Ship Money. England's monarchs had long collected money for ships from certain ports, but Charles extended the obligation to the whole kingdom as payment for national defense. By assessing and taxing the wealth in the inland towns, he stumbled onto a fertile source of income. During these dark days, later referred to by Charles's opponents as "The

Eleven Years of Tyranny," Archbishop Laud carried out the king's religious policies, including the vigorous persecution of Puritans.

This period of Charles's personal rule coincided with a quiet rise in Cromwell's fortunes. He lived a relatively simple life until he inherited a considerable amount of land in eastern England from an uncle in 1636. Now a wealthy man with influential relatives and friends, Cromwell was chosen to represent the town of Cambridge when Charles finally called a meeting of Parliament in 1640.

> *That slovenly fellow [Cromwell] which you see before us, who hath no ornament in his speech; I say that sloven, if we should ever come to have a breach with the King (which God forbid) in such a case will be one of the greatest men of England.*
> —JOHN HAMPDEN
> speaking to fellow M.P.
> Lord Digby in 1629

Cromwell, discouraged by the persecution of Puritans that had marked the reign of James I (1566–1625) and continued under Charles I (1600–49), considered emigrating to the Puritan colony of Massachusetts in 1630. Here, Cromwell is portrayed negotiating passage for himself and his family.

2

The Civil War Begins

> Pax Quaeritur Bello—*Let Peace be sought through War.*
> —OLIVER CROMWELL
> his personal motto

By wisely keeping the country out of foreign wars, Charles managed to rule England without Parliament for 11 years. Without an expensive war on his hands, the king was able to collect enough taxes to finance governmental needs. His problems began when he became too greedy, figuring that if he could successfully control England, there was no reason why he should not have as much power in his two other lands, Ireland and Scotland.

Ireland had been resisting English domination ever since Henry II conquered the island in 1171. To make matters worse, the Irish Catholics refused to accept Anglicanism, England's state religion after the Protestant Reformation in the 16th century. But the resistant Irish Catholics were kept under royal control with the help of Charles's skillful adviser, Sir Thomas Wentworth, the earl of Strafford. Because Strafford so efficiently and so strictly ruled the country, he was known as Ireland's "Black Tom Tyrant."

The situation in Scotland was a different story. The Scots' Presbyterian church symbolized their resistance to Stuart domination. They believed in an egalitarian church that did not grant all governing

THE BETTMANN ARCHIVE

Cromwell, who first sat as a Member of Parliament (M.P.) from 1628 to 1629, gained reelection in 1640. He and his colleagues enacted legislation designed to limit the prerogatives of the king by abolishing several royal courts and declaring illegal all taxation imposed without Parliament's consent.

King Charles I of England, as portrayed by Flemish painter Anthony Van Dyck (1599–1641). Charles's political ineptitude, Catholic sympathies, extreme anti-Puritanism, and fiscal irresponsibility did little to endear him to Parliament, which, in 1640, rejected his request for increased taxation to finance a war with Scotland.

power to a handful of bishops, which is precisely
what they saw going on in the state church. Charles
did not help matters much when he attempted to
establish religious uniformity in the northern kingdom by introducing a prayer book with a decidedly
Catholic slant. This plan backfired, leading to an
armed rebellion. By the beginning of 1639 war had
broken out between the two countries.

But to his dismay, Charles found that he did not
have enough money to fight. Charles's financial situation became even more hopeless when his tax-
payers went on strike, realizing that their once
omnipotent king was clearly threatened by the Scottish army. Charles then tried to bargain with the
Scots, promising to abandon the prayer book that
had incited the rebellion, but the Scots went forward with the war and easily defeated the king's
forces in June 1639.

Desperately in need of supplies, Charles was
forced to turn to Parliament for help. In April 1640
he summoned the first Parliament in 11 years, only
to find out that he would not be granted any money
until he responded to a list of grievances, which
included complaints about his arbitrary methods of
taxation and opposition to the war with the Scots.
Deciding that this body was too troublesome to deal
with, Charles dissolved the session after only three
weeks, hence its name, the Short Parliament.

But the government's position was even more precarious than either Charles or his advisers realized.
A second attempt to defeat the Scots was even more
humiliating than the first. Suffering a crushing defeat on the battlefield, the king was forced to negotiate a cease-fire immediately. The triumphant
Scottish army now occupied the north of England.
It even demanded that the English pay all their
expenses!

Without any other recourse, the thwarted king
had to summon a second Parliament to bail him out
of this hopeless situation. On November 3, 1640,
the Long Parliament (which would sit for 13 years)
began functioning. Before this Parliament's dissolution the political life of England would be trans-
formed by revolutionary change.

But for the time being, Parliament set out to force some drastic changes in Charles's government. Because he was in such dire financial straits, the king was basically powerless. Parliament took advantage of his situation. First off, his two chief advisers, Archbishop William Laud and the earl of Strafford, were arrested. Parliament had long suspected Laud was a papist, disapproving of his habit of promoting bishops to government office. There were more serious complaints against Strafford. Among the crimes he was accused of was raising an army in Ireland that many believed he planned to use against his opponents in England. Since Strafford was considered much more dangerous, he was quickly tried and executed in May 1641. Laud would follow him to the scaffold a few years later.

Parliament then took measures to protect itself from arbitrary royal actions. No longer would a king be able to dissolve a session without Parliament's consent, such as had occurred in 1629. Furthermore, if the king failed to summon a session, Parliament would automatically meet every three years. More measures reducing the king's power, especially regarding taxation and the court system, were also quickly enacted.

Not noted for his debating skills, and inexperienced in legislative matters, Cromwell did not play a major role in the dramatic early months of the Long Parliament. Yet he was strongly supportive of his cousin, John Pym, the most able politician in the House of Commons and leader of the radical group that wished to weaken royal power. At this time Cromwell was mainly interested in religious matters, hoping to eliminate the Anglican church "root and branch." In his only recorded speech during the first few months of Parliament's session, he called for the removal of all bishops holding positions in government, including those who were members of the House of Lords. He later demanded that the parishes be given the right to choose their own ministers.

As Cromwell and his radical colleagues pushed for more measures to ensure that the king could never infringe on their political and religious rights, a

Thomas Wentworth (foreground, in witness stand; 1593–1641), earl of Strafford, is tried before Parliament in May 1641 on charges of having planned to raise a royalist army in Ireland to use against his opponents in England. Cromwell was one of the M.P.s who voted for the earl's execution.

counterreaction arose among the more moderate faction of Parliament. These moderates thought no further changes were necessary now that the king's advisers had been punished and certain reforms enacted, and especially now that the Scottish army had been paid off and sent home. In short, Cromwell and his allies disagreed with the moderates on one major point: they did not trust Charles.

The conflict between the radicals and the moderates became more apparent in October 1641. A rebellion broke out in Ireland, now freed from the heavy hand of Strafford, and the radicals suspected the worst. They imagined that Charles may have helped inspire the rebellion in order to raise an army that he could later use to arrest his English opponents, namely themselves, and then dictate terms to Parliament once again. The question now arose: who would control the army organized to defeat the rebellion, the king or Parliament?

The radicals had reason to doubt Charles's integrity. Not only did he have a tendency to go back on his word, but he was also a cunning manipulator, willing to go to any length for his own gain.

The radicals' fears were realized in January 1642 when Charles, commanding an army unit, marched to the door of the Commons and demanded the arrest of Pym and four other radical leaders. Having been warned in advance, the five members escaped, leaving Charles empty-handed and embarrassed.

After this incident compromise no longer seemed possible. When Charles found out that London and many other parts of the country were rallying in support of the radicals, he and his royal entourage left for safer regions in the north. At once, the country polarized into either supporters of Parliament (small landholders and Protestants) or defenders of the Crown (aristocrats and Anglicans). Open warfare between the two groups seemed inevitable. By the summer of 1642 the king had raised his standard at Nottingham, signaling the start of the first Civil War.

In the early days of the Long Parliament, Cromwell is described as having been a "backbencher," noted mainly for his defense of commoners and his ill-

> *Peace and our liberties are the only thing we aim at; till we have peace I am sure we can enjoy no liberties, and without our liberties I shall not heartily desire peace.*
> —RALPH VERNEY
> member of the House of Commons, calling, in 1642, for war against Charles I

fitting suits. But during the tense months leading up to the outbreak of fighting, he began to move into action. As the parliamentary representative from Cambridge, Cromwell knew that the university owned a valuable silver plate. Since both sides were seizing treasures all over England to help finance their cause, Cromwell suspected that royalist troops would try to obtain the Cambridge silver. Raising an army on his own, he held off an enemy attack and secured the silver for Parliament. Later that month he systematically organized a troop (about 100 men) of cavalry in Huntingdon.

Seventeenth-century armies mainly consisted of footsoldiers, cavalry, and artillery. The footsoldiers were the most abundant, consisting of both pikemen and musketeers. The pikemen were armed with sharp, 16- to 18-foot-long spears; and were protected by a breastplate, backplate, as well as a "pot," or helmet. The musketeers used a "matchlock," one of the first versions of hand-held gunpowder weapons. The matchlock utilized a lighted cord or "match" to set off the charge. Such a weapon was only capable of sending a ball 100 yards and its short reloading capability made the wielder extremely vulnerable against assault after firing. Their only protection was their helmets and the iron spikes called "Swedish feathers" driven into the ground at odd angles to ward off a cavalry charge.

The cavalry were by far the most prestigious of English forces in the 17th century. They were lighter versions of the armored medieval knights of earlier centuries, wearing only a "pot," "breast," and "back." They rode on horseback into battle wielding sabers and firing small matchlock handguns, or "derringers." Their main advantage was quick maneuverability and the devastating effect of the charging horse crashing into men on foot.

Artillery of the day was restricted to great iron cannons that were either attached to castle turrets or dragged into battle upon horse-drawn carts.

It was not considered unusual for a man with Cromwell's lack of military experience to assume military command. As a respected member of the gentry and a recognized radical, he was expected to

In January 1642 Charles I entered the House of Commons to arrest five of his most radical and outspoken critics only to discover that his enemies had been warned and had fled to safety. Realizing that his influence with Parliament was now negligible and that war was inevitable, the king left London to seek assistance from his supporters in northern and western England.

exercise leadership. There were very few professional soldiers in England, and a majority of those fought on the royalist side. Thus, any man of wealth willing to organize a parliamentary troop was encouraged to do so.

The inexperience of Parliament's forces, however, was one of the reasons the war dragged on so long. What set Cromwell apart from the rest was the speed with which he learned his responsibilities and the aggressive way he took command. For example, at a time when Parliament still blamed the conflict not on the king, but on his advisers, Cromwell spoke otherwise. He bluntly told his men that if the king should charge him in battle he would shoot him as he would anyone else.

What Parliament lacked in experience it made up in numbers, drawing support from the more industrialized, populous southern and eastern parts of the country. If the royalists hoped to win the war, they would quickly have to take the initiative, before Parliament had a chance to organize its forces.

Charles made his move in October 1642. A royal army began to march toward London, Parliament's

The conflict known as the first English Civil War commenced on August 25, 1642, when Charles I raised his standard at Nottingham Castle. A contemporary observer wrote of the unprepared troops: ". . . the whole business of fighting was . . . chiefly performed by untravelled gentlemen, raw citizens, and generals that had scarce ever before seen a battle."

main center. If they could capture London with this one blow, the war might be over. The commander of this army was Charles's nephew, Prince Rupert.

The royal soldiers called themselves Cavaliers, a name derived from the French word *chevalier*, meaning gallant and aristocratic. Rupert — a dashing, romantic figure with military experience in German wars — epitomized the name more than anyone else. "Roundheads," the nickname given to their lower-class opponents, had a derisive ring, referring to their short haircuts. At the time fashionable aristocrats wore their hair in long curls.

The first great battle of the Civil War took place at Edgehill on October 23, 1642. The Roundheads, led by Robert Devereux, third earl of Essex, blocked Rupert's march to London. The two armies of approximately equal strength — 20,000 infantrymen and 5,000 cavalry — faced each other. Using typical battle formations of the day, the infantry units took their place in the center, with cavalry placed on each side. The battle started with a charge by Rupert's cavalry.

The Cavalier cavalry attacked so ferociously that the left side of the Roundhead army crumbled and started to flee in panic. But instead of turning on what was left of Essex's infantry, Rupert's relentless horsemen continued to chase the retreating enemy cavalry. Their overzealous pursuit left Rupert's infantry exposed to a severe counterattack by the Roundheads. By the time Rupert's horsemen finally returned to the battlefield, night had fallen and the fighting was over.

Both sides claimed victory at Edgehill, despite its inconclusive nature. Nevertheless, Parliament managed to keep the Cavaliers from capturing London. Charles then retired to Oxford, which became his capital city for the duration of the war.

Cromwell had been present during the Battle of Edgehill. His Huntingdon troop had been held in reserve, and was only called upon during the successful counterattack. While he waited on the sideline Cromwell had watched the course of action very carefully, drawing important conclusions from what he had witnessed. The spirit of Rupert's cav-

Prince Rupert (1619–82), count Palatine of Rhine, was appointed general of cavalry by Charles I in 1641. Though Rupert was a capable commander, the disorderliness of his cavalry at the Battle of Edgehill in October 1642 convinced Cromwell that strict military discipline might prove to be the key to a parliamentary victory.

Scottish religious reformer John Knox (1513–72) was a leading exponent of Calvinism, an austere form of Protestantism named for its originator, French theologian John Calvin (1509–64). Cromwell's Calvinist convictions — whereby he considered himself chosen for salvation — contributed to the confidence of spirit that distinguished his career.

alry truly impressed him, but he also noted that those horsemen did not stop charging their retreating opponents when it no longer served a rational military purpose. To Cromwell's Puritan mind, these royalists lacked discipline, an essential ingredient when carrying out complicated maneuvers in the midst of battle. He knew that if Parliament could somehow raise an army of dedicated and disciplined men, victory over the king could be achieved.

With this idea in mind, Cromwell returned home in the winter to help organize an association of five counties in the east of England (two more would join the following year), which formed the Eastern Association Army. This army raised more troops than any other comparable area in England.

In the process of bringing the Eastern Association Army together, Cromwell was able to increase the size of his own unit, bringing it up to regiment strength. By March 1643 he had his first regiment formed into five troops. By September it had grown to 14 troops or 1,400 men under his command. For his service in raising so many men, Cromwell was promoted from captain to colonel early in the year.

Although he rapidly expanded the size of his units, Cromwell selected his troops very carefully, looking for certain qualities in his soldiers — discipline and dedication.

Cromwell enforced discipline among his men by giving them strict rules to abide by. The parliamentarian newspaper *Special Passages* stated that Colonel Cromwell had "2,000 brave men, well disciplined; no man swears but he pays his twelve pence; if he be drunk he is set in the stocks, or worse, if one calls the other 'Roundhead' he is cashiered [dishonorably discharged]. . . . How happy it were if all the forces were thus disciplined." He absolutely expected his men to obey orders. When two men attempted to desert early in the war, Cromwell used them as an example and had them publicly whipped.

To obtain dedicated fighters in his units, Cromwell tried to accept only religious men, believing that their enthusiasm for serving God would make them spirited and courageous soldiers. It did not matter to him that many of these men adhered to sects sometimes considered fanatical, for Cromwell knew that religious fervor could easily be converted into martial fervor. "I have lovely company," he told a friend, "You would respect them did you know them; they are no Anabaptists [an extreme Protestant sect]; they are honest, sober Christians."

Another wise innovation by Cromwell was to promote officers according to their proven ability. He upset his moderate colleagues by deliberately ignoring the practice of the day that tended to give high rank only to rich men. A fellow commander once described Cromwell's officers as "common men, poor and of mean parentage."

Cromwell's disciplined and dedicated fighting force had its first test of strength in May 1643. Near the town of Grantham in Lincolnshire, his army found itself face to face with a royalist army twice its size. After exchanging musketfire for about a half hour, Cromwell decided to take the initiative. He ordered his men to charge, surprising their opponents, who immediately fled the battlefield. Losing only two men and killing nearly 100 of the enemy, Cromwell achieved an impressive first victory. It was totally in character for this modest Puritan to at-

I had rather have a plain russet-coated captain that knows what he fights for, and loves what he knows, than that which you call a gentleman and is nothing else. I honour a gentleman that is so indeed.
—OLIVER CROMWELL
speaking in August 1643

King's College, Cambridge University, whose silver was expropriated by Cromwell to finance the parliamentary war effort. Cromwell threw himself into preparing for the conflict, selecting men who ". . . would as one man stand firmly."

ART RESOURCE

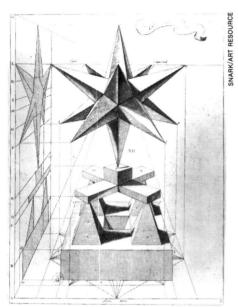

A geometrical drawing dating from the mid-17th century, when England's Puritan scholars were rapidly emerging as their country's intellectual leaders. Cromwell greatly esteemed this new, experimental spirit in science, which some historians consider an extension of the Puritan quest for personal religious experience.

tribute his success to the powerful hand of the Lord: "God hath given us, this evening, a glorious victory over our enemies." That same hand would grant him many more triumphs.

Throughout the rest of the summer Cromwell added several more victories to his credit. One of his greatest triumphs occurred at Gainsborough. Although he was forced to retreat, Cromwell demonstrated that he had mastered sophisticated leadership skills.

While facing a large royalist army, Cromwell was surprised by yet another massive royalist cavalry. But Cromwell maintained control over his men and managed to lead them away from danger. In Cromwell's own words: "With some difficulty we got our horse [cavalry] into a body, and with them forced the enemy and retreated in such good order that though the enemy followed hard, yet they were not able to disorder us, but we got them off safe to Lincoln." Many experts in military strategy regard this safe orderly retreat as a masterly exercise, for by keeping his men under control Cromwell avoided a possible massacre. Even though he did not win this battle, it is ranked with his greatest victories.

By the end of the summer Cromwell had been named one of the chief colonels in the Eastern Association Army, now under the command of Edward Montagu, second earl of Manchester. Despite Cromwell's outstanding performance, Parliament was losing the war. Other generals had not matched Cromwell's successes. Also, serious financial problems made it difficult to supply the armies. At times, in order to keep up the morale of his troops, Cromwell paid his men out of his own coffers. Added to these insecurities were rumors that the king was trying to bring in troops from Ireland.

Parliament desperately needed to strengthen its military position. It looked to Scotland for help, and began negotiating an alliance in the summer of 1643. The Scots, fearing a royalist victory over Parliament, were prepared to enter the war. Their well-tested army, having defeated Charles in the past, would bolster parliamentary forces at a time when the king seemed to be gaining the upper hand. Parliament needed outside support so badly that it promised the Scots that the future religious settlement in England would conform to Scottish Presbyterianism, which tended to be rigid and intolerant, with no diversities of church practice permitted.

Cromwell had mixed feelings about this new alliance. He was troubled about the effect the Scots would have on the future religious settlement in England, but he recognized the need for military assistance. He therefore decided to keep his objections to himself. Besides, he had other things to worry about.

Cromwell's proven military capabilities had not gone unnoticed. In January 1644 Cromwell had obtained commission as lieutenant general of the Eastern Association Army. He thus devoted his energies to the new campaigns scheduled to begin in the spring.

When spring arrived the Scottish army had linked up with Manchester and Cromwell. With a joint army numbering 25,000 men, they set out to overthrow an important royalist force at York. To relieve this siege Charles sent his best general, Prince Rupert. After Rupert easily freed the royalist forces at York, he left to link up with a larger royalist contingent. He did not get far, for barring his way were

ALINARI/ART RESOURCE

A Van Dyck portrait shows three of Charles I's children: Charles (left; 1630–85), prince of Wales (the future King Charles II); James (center; 1633–1701), duke of York (the future King James II); and Princess Elizabeth (1636–50).

the combined Scottish and parliamentary armies.

Rupert had earlier asked a Roundhead soldier who had been captured and released if Cromwell was present on the other side. When the soldier answered affirmatively, Rupert vowed to place his forces directly opposite Cromwell. After hearing the soldier's story, Cromwell replied, "By God's grace, he shall have fighting enough."

On July 2, 1644, the two armies met at Marston Moor. This important battle began with Cromwell's cavalry leading the way. From both sides the steady chant of psalms rose into the air, a familiar background sound to the campaigns of the Civil War. The cavalry broke through the royalist ranks and advanced into the line of reserves. In the hand-to-hand combat that ensued, Cromwell was wounded in the neck by a pistol shot fired at such close range that he was temporarily blinded by the flash of exploding gunpowder. Though stunned and momentarily incapacitated, he refused to leave the battlefield. Cromwell even managed to regroup his men and attack the royalist cavalry again from the rear when part of Parliament's army under Sir Thomas Fairfax faltered. In the meantime, the Scots chased the remaining royalist cavalry from the field. This final stage of the battle proved short and decisive. Royalist troops scattered, some of them fleeing all the way back to York.

The Battle of Marston Moor was a great triumph for Parliament. Three to four thousand Cavaliers had been killed and about one thousand taken prisoner. A couple of days later York fell to the Roundheads as well, adding dimension to the victory. When news of the battle reached London, most accounts singled out Cromwell as the chief agent in bringing about victory. Some reports actually referred to him as the "savior of the three kingdoms." Cromwell modestly dismissed these acclaims. As always, he attributed Parliament's success as "a great favor from God."

Another compliment came unexpectedly from Rupert's men. Recognizing his steadfastness in battle, they began calling him "Ironside." Since his greatness was reflected in his troops, eventually the term

That Cromwell was recognized as the architect of the victory at Marston Moor displeased Parliament's Presbyterian Scottish allies, who considered Cromwell and all other non-Presbyterians godless "Independents."

"Ironsides" was applied to his soldiers as well.

Despite the nickname, Cromwell had a more sensitive side to his personality. When he wrote a note of sympathy to his brother-in-law after his nephew was killed at Marston Moor, Cromwell mourned the loss of his own two sons, Oliver and Robert. "You know my trials this way," he wrote in this touching letter, "but the Lord supported me with this: that the Lord took him [his nephew] into the happiness we all pant for and live for. There is your precious child full of glory, to know sin nor sorrow no more."

The war and bloodshed continued. After the fall of York, however, something strange began to happen. With a complete victory now so close at hand, Manchester did not appear in any great hurry to press his military advantage. In fact, it seemed like the general did not want to win any more victories over the royalists. At one point Manchester even threatened to hang one of his officers who captured a royalist castle without first asking his permission.

Cromwell, his right arm rendered useless by wounds received in an earlier engagement, leads a troop of cavalry into action at the Battle of Marston Moor in 1644. Cromwell's expert handling of the cavalry resulted in a resounding parliamentary victory and further added to his growing reputation as a gifted commander.

Cromwell had to intervene to save the officer's life.

Manchester had stopped seeking Cromwell's advice on military strategy, but Cromwell continued to try to prod the general into taking more aggressive action. Manchester would not listen: "If we beat the king 99 times, yet he is king still . . . but if the king best us once we shall all be hanged." Cromwell did not understand his rationale. "Why did we take up arms at first," he argued. "This is against fighting ever hereafter; if so let us make peace, be it never so base."

Manchester's behavior became increasingly worrisome as the royalists recovered from their setbacks and seriously defeated Essex in September 1644. In many ways this success helped nullify Cromwell's great victories at Marston Moor and York. Manchester's reluctance to campaign vigorously provided the king with new opportunities.

Now there was no denying the fact that Manchester was trying to avoid a complete victory over the king. Why he changed his attitude towards the war has never been satisfactorily explained. Most likely, he sided with those parliamentary moderates who preferred a negotiated rather than a dictated peace with the king. That way the king would be allowed to share in political power with Parliament.

The leading threat to Manchester's scheme was Cromwell, his own lieutenant. Never one to sit by passively when he saw something going awry, Cromwell began to complain publicly about Manchester's "slowness in all things." Unlike Manchester, Cromwell refused to compromise with the king. He favored a radical final settlement. Not trusting Charles, he sought to make Parliament the major institution in the kingdom. Cromwell would never settle for a final arrangement that gave Charles an opportunity to once again establish an absolute monarchy in England. To prevent this from happening the Cavaliers would have to be convincingly defeated on the battlefield.

The dispute between the two generals spread to London, where Parliament's leaders tried to get the two men to reconcile their differences. But despite a patched-up agreement in September, Manches-

Cromwell was rather well set than tall, strong and robustuous of constitution, of visage leonine—the true physiognomy of all great and martial men.
—ROBERT FLECKNOE
17th-century British poet
and biographer of Cromwell

ter's pattern of half-heartedly pursuing the war continued. In October 1644 he finally allowed his army to engage in combat in the Battle of Newbury. But the outcome proved inconclusive, mainly because at a key moment Manchester hesitated to give the command to attack. After the fighting was over, Manchester allowed the royalists to recover vital arms and artillery that could have been captured.

Cromwell and Manchester were now at each others' throats. Returning to Parliament in November, Cromwell made his feelings about Manchester and his inept strategies known. He delivered a blistering speech, blaming Manchester for every mishap that had befallen Parliament's army since the taking of York the past July. Cromwell argued that the roots of their present difficulties lay in the general's unwillingness to achieve a complete victory over the king. Although he focused on Manchester, he was actually condemning all those generals, including Essex, who wished for a compromise settlement with the royalists.

When Manchester rose to defend himself, he used the occasion to discredit his accuser. He said that Cromwell was trying to subvert basic institutions. For example, Cromwell was alleged to have spoken against nobility, saying that he hoped never again to see a nobleman in England. And he was reported to have expressed hostility towards Parliament's allies, the Scots, and their religious practices.

Interestingly, Cromwell never denied these charges. He was an impulsive person, and in the heat of an argument it is likely that he did make such remarks. He definitely disliked the intolerant nature of Scottish Presbyterianism, and very likely he was also suspicious of the English aristocracy, most of whom either actively supported the king or, at best, held rather moderate views.

At this point, an inquiry by Parliament to find out why the war had been going so badly now turned into a political squabble. A majority in the House of Lords defended Manchester, while the more radical members of the Commons supported Cromwell. Unless these differences could somehow be resolved, an end to the war was nowhere in sight.

A wounded royalist raises his pistol as parliamentary cavalrymen bear down upon him at the Battle of Marston Moor. The steadfastness that Cromwell displayed earned him the admiration and respect of his royalist opponents, who began calling him "Ironside," a term that was later applied to the troopers he commanded as well.

3

New Model Army

As Cromwell grew to place and authority, his parts seemed to be renewed, as if he had concealed faculties till he had the occasion to use them.
—EDWARD HYDE
1st Earl of Clarendon, in his
History of the Great Rebellion,
published in 1702

The dispute between the two generals, Manchester and Cromwell, called into question a fundamental aspect of parliamentary politics: what would be the exact nature of the settlement with the king? More immediately, it raised the question of how the war should be conducted. Nothing could be accomplished as long as Parliament's leaders — many of whom were also commanders in the army — continued to tie themselves up in disagreements.

Suddenly, in December 1644, when the quarrel between the moderate and radical members of Parliament was reaching its peak, Cromwell let the matter drop, stating: "Therefore waving a strict inquiry into the causes of these things, let us apply ourselves to the remedy, which is most necessary. And I hope we have such true English hearts, and zealous affections towards the general weal of our Mother Country, as no Members of either House will scruple to deny themselves, and their own private interest, for the public good. . . . " Soon after, a solution was introduced in the House of Commons. This solution rescued Parliament from the fate of being indefinitely split into two opposing factions.

THE BETTMANN ARCHIVE

A Puritan clergyman here preaches to parliamentary troops. The Puritans' conviction that God was on their side accounts for the unshakable self-righteousness and immense self-assurance that characterized their endeavors to overthrow the established order.

Cromwell peers down at a portrait of Charles I. Even the image of England's king became disturbing to many parliamentary supporters during the English Civil War.

King Gustavus II Adolphus (1594–1632) of Sweden, one of the most brilliant generals of his day, supported the Protestant princes of Europe against their Catholic enemies. Some of the officers on both sides in the English Civil War had gained experience fighting with Gustavus's armies.

Although the Puritans lived by a code of humility, it was a Presbyterian member, Zouch Tate, who blamed all the recent conflicts on "pride and covetousness." Tate made a motion to call all members of Parliament to resign their positions in the army. This was the famous Self-Denying Ordinance, which seemed to provide the magic formula by which all the current troubles affecting Parliament might disappear. With one swift blow, all the squabbling officers, including Cromwell, Manchester and Essex, would quickly be removed from the scene.

The House of Lords opposed this measure, complaining that nobles would be automatically eliminated from positions of influence. Nevertheless, the feeling in Parliament was that sacrifices would have to be made. The Self-Denying Ordinance was passed by the Commons 10 days after it was introduced. The House of Lords would give in to the measure a few months later.

Cromwell enthusiastically supported the ordinance, even though it meant that he would have to retire as a soldier. Perhaps he believed that his own sacrifice would be a small price to pay for new generals who would fight the war to a victorious end.

The Self-Denying Ordinance gave rise to the New Model Army. As soon as the measure was enacted, Parliament set out to reorganize the military. A reform was urgently needed, for the army had nearly disintegrated. The troops were terribly demoralized and large numbers of soldiers had deserted. Those who remained suffered severe hardships, mainly because Parliament had difficulty arranging for pay and supplies. In a speech on December 9 Cromwell said that "till the whole army were new modelled and governed under a stricter discipline, they must not expect any notable success in anything they were about." To combat this problem Parliament decided that the new army would be funded by regular, assured taxes. This new modeling of the military was essential if Parliament hoped to establish a military force that could effectively engage the royalists in the spring campaign.

The New Model Army consisted of 22,000 men of horse and foot, broken down into three armies of approximately 8,000 soldiers each. Discipline was achieved by utilizing the same rules that Cromwell had introduced among his Ironsides. The New Model Army would be a national army loyal to Parliament alone. The infighting between the various and independent provincial forces became a thing of the past. To further unify the army, all troops were outfitted in red. "Redcoats all," a newspaper called the New Model Army.

Since the earl of Essex had been removed by the Self-Denying Ordinance, a new commander in chief for the New Model Army had to be appointed. Parliament chose Sir Thomas Fairfax, an officer who had fought with Cromwell in the Battle of Marston Moor. Not at all personally ambitious or flamboyant, Fairfax was recommended because he was a dedicated soldier, committed to victory, who wished to avoid political controversy. Cromwell knew his vir-

Parliamentary troops ransack the house of a royalist nobleman. As a military leader, Cromwell thought confiscating royalist property a justifiable means of financing the parliamentary war effort. As a landowner, however, he abhorred the beliefs of Puritan radicals who were against property ownership.

Charles I rallies his cavalry at the Battle of Naseby, June 14, 1645. The crushing defeat that Cromwell's New Model Army inflicted on the royalists at Naseby included a political bonus — in the baggage abandoned by the king in his escape was correspondence that revealed he had been negotiating to secure military assistance from the French and the Irish.

tues and therefore gave very strong support to Fairfax's nomination. A major general named Phillip Skippon was selected to lead the infantry. But for some mysterious reason Cromwell's old position of lieutenant general of the cavalry remained vacant.

Years later, Cromwell's enemies suggested that he and his radical allies engineered the creation of the New Model Army with the intention of placing Cromwell in the empty slot. But there is no direct evidence to support these charges. Nevertheless, of all the generals who were members of Parliament, only Cromwell managed to keep his position, for he even-

tually resumed his command of the cavalry.

When the House of Lords finally passed the Self-Denying Ordinance on April 3, 1645, it did so with the provision that officers might take up to 40 days to relinquish their commands. Earlier in February, when news came that royalist troops threatened the west of England, Parliament had ordered Cromwell's old regiments to join General William Waller, the western commander. But many of these soldiers rebelled and refused to follow orders. At that point Parliament requested Cromwell to step in and discipline his troops. Since his soldiers had a special affection for Cromwell, they instantly obeyed him. Together with Waller's men they were able to subdue the royalist threat. Waller, who was soon to give up his own commission, went out of his way to praise Cromwell's loyalty and his willingness to follow the direction of superior officers.

Cromwell's commission had still not expired, so Parliament sent him back to the battlefield in April to prevent the king from linking up his army with Prince Rupert's forces. Cromwell succeeded in this task, seizing ammunition, horses, and muskets at the key royal fortress of Bletchingdon House, due to "the prudence or cowardice" of its commander, who did not give battle. Once more he attributed his success to God: "This was the mercy of God and nothing more than a real acknowledgement."

On April 19 Cromwell returned to the New Model Army's headquarters at Windsor to surrender his commission. But the next day a letter arrived from Parliament, giving him fresh assignments. The king's major army had been taking the field, prepared for an active campaign.

Unfortunately, the New Model Army was in no condition to provide adequate opposition. The reorganization process had taken longer than expected, and many details had yet to be worked out — including the naming of an officer to fill the empty position. In the end the army would be left better paid, better managed, and better supplied, but for the time being it was still in a state of disarray. It was an unknown force, inexperienced and untested. The king and his generals ridiculed the New

Charles, prince of Wales, as portrayed by William Dobson (1610–46). King Charles I became increasingly concerned for his son's safety as it became apparent that Parliament would win the war. The prince was sent to England's remote West Country region, from where he might escape abroad in the event of his father's capture.

> *Freedom of religion was not the thing at first contested for, but God brought it to that issue at last . . . and at last it proved that which was most dear to us.*
>
> —OLIVER CROMWELL
> reflecting on the goals of
> the first Civil War

This 1647 Anglican broadsheet identifies tradesmen as prominent propagandists for radical Puritanism. One historian suggests that their radicalism can be partially attributed to the talkativeness prevalent in ". . . sedentary trades in which conversation is a natural accompaniment to work."

Model Army, nicknaming it the "New Noodle Army."

The royalists took immediate advantage of their opponents' disorganization by capturing the city of Leicester. Fairfax had been instructed to seek out the king and force a major battle, but he reacted hesitantly. He felt uneasy about going into combat without a competent commander for his cavalry. On June 10 Fairfax petitioned Parliament for Cromwell to assume this position, arguing that no one else would do. "The general esteem and affection which he hath both with the officers and soldiers of this whole army, his own personal worth and ability," according to Fairfax, made Cromwell indispensable. When the Commons approved a temporary extension of the deadline, Fairfax sent for Cromwell immediately.

As Cromwell rode into the army camp on June 13, he was greeted with cries of "Ironsides has come to lead us!" His presence quickly bolstered the morale of the troops. Surprisingly, the king's forces still remained confident of victory. They were well aware of Cromwell's military genius, but believed that Parliament's army, having been racked with squabbles, no longer had the necessary discipline. They even minimized Cromwell's earlier contributions. When he heard reports of their predictions of victory, Cromwell smiled. Some even swore that he carried that smile into battle the next day, when the Royalists and the New Model Army came face to face at Naseby.

The Battle of Naseby on June 14, 1645, demonstrated that the New Model Army had overcome its difficulties. The royalists made a strong showing at first, as Rupert's cavalry charged through Parliament's left lines. But as had happened at Edgehill, Rupert's men continued their advance far beyond the field. In fact, they chased the enemy two miles away. In the meantime, Cromwell, as usual, kept his men completely under control. He wheeled his cavalry around and attacked the now exposed royalist infantry. In short, these foot soldiers were massacred. By the time Rupert's men decided to return to the field, the Cavaliers had already lost. When they saw that the New Model Army had destroyed their infantry and taken command, they turned and fled in fear.

The king was totally defeated by the army he once ridiculed. Not only had he lost all his infantry and all his guns, he had lost valuable baggage as well. This included chests that contained jewels and gems, as well as his private papers and correspondence, much of it incriminating and embarrassing. Some of these letters were published, including those that revealed Charles's double-dealing with Irish papists. Proof that the king was trying to bring in Catholic troops from Ireland certainly weakened the case of those who still trusted Charles and sought to work out an agreement with him.

In his report to Parliament, Cromwell once again attributed his success to God. But this time, even more boldly, he praised the men in the army, pleading that these brave souls deserved liberty of conscience in their religious practices. The House of Commons printed Cromwell's letter, but the line urging religious toleration was cautiously removed. Some of the members of the House of Commons felt that such words would offend their Scottish allies and the more conservative members of Parliament. But deleted or not, Cromwell had established the principle that he and his men regarded religious freedom as one of the main reasons they were fighting this war.

Following on the heels of the Naseby battle came the Battle of Long Sutton near Langport in July. Smaller in scale, it still offered evidence of the bravery and tight discipline of Cromwell's soldiers. This time, the Ironside cavalry had to charge up a very narrow pass towards a position strongly defended by the enemy. With this victory under its belt, the New Model Army appeared invincible.

In many ways the Naseby and Langport battles represented the crowning successes of the first Civil War. The remaining battles consisted of brief skirmishes. In December, after a particularly humiliating defeat for Rupert, Cromwell sent off another message to Parliament calling for religious freedom. And once again, the offending passages were removed before the letter was published, giving a good

> *I could not riding alone about my business, but smile out to God in praises, in assurance of victory because God would, by things that are not, bring to naught things that are.*
> —OLIVER CROMWELL
> before the Battle of Naseby

Charles I's wife, Queen Henrietta Maria (1609–69), a French princess by birth, was an extremely devout Catholic. The fact that the king tolerated her thinly disguised contempt for Anglicanism and allowed himself to be persuaded by her to pursue a pro-Catholic foreign policy was a major cause of the hatred that many of his subjects felt toward him.

English poet John Milton (1608–74), a staunch supporter of the parliamentary cause, was, like Cromwell (whom he knew personally), convinced that the English were God's "chosen people."

indication of how Parliament would react once the war was over and the soldiers came forth to demand the rights they had fought for.

On June 20, 1646, with the surrender of the king's headquarters at Oxford, the war came to an end. But when Parliament came to collect Charles, it found that the king had fled from the city. When he realized that his military position had become hopeless, he escaped from Oxford and turned himself over to the Scots, hoping that the Scottish army would protect him from the English if he pretended to accept their version of Presbyterianism. Charles loved to play the game of dividing his enemies in order to conquer them. Believing he could turn the Scots against Parliament, Charles hoped to avoid a radical settlement that would strip him of his power. At the same time, he made overtures to Cromwell's soldiers, implying that he would grant England freedom of religion.

Charles's various secret negotiations were full of false promises and contradictory offers. Perhaps

this is the reason Cromwell publicly rebuked those officers who wished to negotiate separately with the king, fearing that Parliament would not force the king to accept a radical settlement. Cromwell did not want to see the king share political power with Parliament either, but he insisted, rather forcefully, that only Parliament could reach a set settlement, and that the army had no right to engage in politics. In a year's time, however, he would alter this view.

By now Cromwell had established quite a reputation for himself. He was considered to be the most outstanding general on either side during the Civil War. Justly appreciated by his men as a valuable commander, he was held in special esteem. Undoubtedly his military prestige contributed to his political prominence, for he was also considered one of the key leaders of the Long Parliament. When he finally discharged his military commission in July, in belated conformity with the terms of the Self-Denying Ordinance, he would take on an even greater political role.

Citizens flee the city to escape the plague. The bubonic plague, called the Black Death, was transmitted by fleas carried on rats that infested cities of earlier times. In the 14th century the plague was responsible for destroying one-fourth of the population of Europe.

4
Levellers

When the first Civil War ended in 1646 and the services of the soldiers were no longer needed, Parliament looked forward to disbanding the New Model Army. It was very expensive for the government to maintain a large force, but the main reason Parliament wanted to be rid of it was because the conservative majority both feared and disliked the army, which consisted of a number of political and religious radicals. Parliament's fears were not unfounded, for these radicals were not about to allow the conservative members to reach a compromising settlement with the king, undermining the freedoms they had fought for. Nor were they about to disband before Parliament made provisions to pay them.

These rumblings in the army later became a roar, with Cromwell at the helm. But for the first few months after the war, Cromwell kept a low profile, spending time with personal, rather than political matters. He moved his family from Ely to London. In January his favorite daughter, Elizabeth, married a wealthy landholder. Then in June, Bridget, the eldest girl, married Commissary General Henry Ireton, Cromwell's most trusted adviser. Two sons

A 17th-century engraving shows the *Sovereign of the Seas*, a warship built for the Royal Navy in 1637. Cromwell's ardent advocacy of the expansion of English seapower resulted in the dominance of the English navy and merchant marine from the Baltic Sea to the Mediterranean Sea.

Cromwell drills his troopers during the closing stages of the first Civil War, which ended when Charles I took refuge with the Scots in mid-1646. During the next one and a half years, Cromwell was preoccupied with defusing the threat posed to the unity of the New Model Army by the agitation of its radical, egalitarian members, known as the Levellers.

had already died, while the two other sons served in the army.

Cromwell, having given up his military commission, was now more involved in parliamentary matters. But he did not particularly enjoy the role of a politician. The art of compromising, and the need for extensive negotiations and meetings frustrated him. As an active person, he wanted quick and decisive results. Parliamentary politics did not provide a proper outlet for a man with his energy and impatience.

From the end of January to the beginning of April 1647, he did not even attend the regular daily sessions of the House of Commons. The stated reason for his absences was an illness, vaguely diagnosed as "an imposture in the head." No doubt Cromwell had become increasingly despondent over recent political developments, so this rather strange ailment probably resulted from his mental condition.

Cromwell was feeling increasingly depressed about how the crucial issues concerning the settlement of the country had begun to take shape during the winter of 1646–47. The moderate group of politicians that had taken over parliamentary leadership strove to work out a peace treaty with the uncooperative king, who kept insisting that his former powers be preserved, even though he had lost the war. Cromwell, along with the radical soldiers, feared that this conservative Parliament would grant the king too many concessions.

Cromwell did not think that Charles should be able to resume where he had left off before the Civil War began in 1642; too much blood had been shed. But he never even considered a republican form of government, having no king.

A new extremist political movement that had emerged during the last few years of the Civil War advocated the only truly democratic formula for the country. The handful of people belonging to the movement were known as *Levellers* because they wished to "level" all social ranks, making everyone equal under the same law. They wanted to do away with the aristocracy as well as the king. But Levellers did not advocate making everyone equal in terms of

THE BETTMANN ARCHIVE

A 17th-century English cartoon likens the negotiations between Charles I (left) and Parliament to a game of chess. In July 1647 Cromwell asserted that it would be very difficult ". . . to introduce a popular government against the King and his party."

You have done your work, and may go to play, unless you will fall out among yourselves.
—JACOB ASTLEY
captured royalist addressing Cromwell's troops, warning prophetically of dissension

wealth, as their critics claimed, for they appreciated the value of private property. This point separated them from the *Diggers*, an even more radical group that advocated sovereignty of the people. They believed that political power in England should be held by the entire adult male population, which would express its will through the ballot. The government would then carry out the will of the majority. At the time, such democratic notions were considered dangerous and subversive, even to a radical such as Cromwell.

Parliament's most recent peace proposal was decidedly more conservative than the Levellers' proposals, but it did call for Charles to give up a good deal of his royal authority. Parliament proposed shifting political power from the king to Parliament, so that the two Houses would essentially run the country in the king's name. But these propositions required Charles's approval, which he refused to give.

While Parliament's leaders tried in vain to come up with an agreement that Charles would approve, he continued to play games with them. Sometimes he pretended that he might consent, then suddenly would reject all proposals looking for better arrangements. One of his favorite tactics was to disrupt the unity of the different factions. He would draw a group, like the Scots, into secret negotiations with him without any serious intention of reaching an agreement. The other factions would get word about the secret meeting thus leading to their fear of conspiracy. Charles was not a person to be trusted, yet the frustrating reality seemed to be that there was no alternative to dealing with him. The Levellers' proposals to do away with the king altogether seemed too drastic — for now.

Parliament appeared to gain the upper hand in January 1647. The king had surrendered himself to the Scots after the war, but they gave up hope of converting him to their Presbyterianism and handed him over to Parliament. Despite this change of captors, Charles kept up his behind-the-scene dealings, continuing his attempts to win over Parliament's army.

Abandoned by the Scots in January 1647 for his refusal to convert to Presbyterianism, Charles I was taken prisoner by Parliament six months later. In the ensuing negotiations, Cromwell displayed a conciliatory attitude that did not sit well with his more radical colleagues.

On the face of it, Charles's negotiations with the army should not have gotten very far, considering that it was an agency of Parliament, not an independent body. Recent events, however, had made the soldiers rather disgruntled and a wave of unrest began sweeping through the rank and file.

What provoked the agitation in the army was mainly its treatment by Parliament, now more completely under the control of conservative politicians. Known as Presbyterians, these conservatives wished to adopt a form of Scottish Presbyterianism in England. This naturally offended the various religious factions in the army that had been recruited by Cromwell, and that had fought so courageously during the Civil War. They opposed the establishment of such a strict, disciplinarian church, especially because it did not allow congregations to choose and support their own ministers.

What provoked the army most of all was Parliament's decision to disband the force without making provision for back pay long owed to the soldiers, many of whom had not been paid for almost a year. Nor did Parliament see fit to offer pensions for the

A Dutch cartoon shows Cromwell receiving a deputation of Levellers in 1647. In July of that year Cromwell gave in to Leveller demands that their Presbyterian opponents in Parliament be removed from power, but when Leveller activism threatened to divide the army, Cromwell ordered one of the ringleaders executed and 11 others imprisoned.

widows and orphans of those killed in the war. At the same time, Parliament tried to crush any plans for an organized revolt by demoting all senior officers, except for General Fairfax, to the rank of colonel. It also passed a measure reinforcing the Self-Denying Ordinance, stating unequivocally that no member of Parliament could serve in the army.

This last enactment was unmistakably aimed at Cromwell. It represented a direct affront to him, and obviously contributed to his sense of frustration. Rumors spread that he considered leaving for the continent to fight for the Protestant cause in the Thirty Years' War. Surely his enemies would have liked to see Cromwell depart. But although he was at first depressed about the treatment of the army, a turn of events opened up a whole new opportunity to demand a more forceful policy against the king.

The conservatives' attempts to disband the army backfired. The soldiers, resenting their unfair treatment, began to rebel. Parliament then tried to get rid of them by suggesting that they volunteer to fight in Ireland, which was still in a state of rebellion, but they refused to go unless Cromwell commanded them. The soldiers were angry at Parliament for depriving them of their favorite officer, but the issue that provoked them more than any other was the sense of injustice created by Parliament's failure to pay them what they deserved. Feeling unappreciated for their great sacrifices, the common soldiers became receptive to the extreme political ideas of the Levellers, then circulating in the poorer areas of London.

It is not surprising that the democratic ideas of the Levellers spread from the poor people of London to the poor troops in the army. Here were political ideas that spoke to the average soldier, now feeling angry and unappreciated. By March 1647 the rank and file of the army appointed delegates, known as "Agitators," to represent the Leveller point of view. Petitions presenting long lists of grievances were drawn up and sent to Parliament.

At first, Parliament was simply annoyed by these rumblings in the army. It accused the Agitators and the signers of the petitions of being enemies of the

> *It is a blessed thing to die daily, for what is there in this world to be accounted of . . .*
> —OLIVER CROMWELL writing in 1647, while in the midst of a deep depression

Lieutenant General Henry Ireton (1611–51) was a gifted politician and soldier whose advice on constitutional matters Cromwell found indispensable. Ireton's *Heads of Proposals*, a program for constitutional reform, was not radical enough for the Levellers.

state and threatened to take strong actions against them. But the army knew that it could easily over-throw Parliament and refused to be bluffed into sub-mission. Talk of mutiny was heard for the first time.

When the leaders of Parliament realized that in-timidation would not work against the army, they tried to work out a compromise. Rather belatedly, they spoke of meeting the army's demands, includ-ing supplying some of the back pay. But their offer proved to be too little and too late. The potential mutiny grew as some of the officers started to join forces with the rank and file.

In May 1647 Parliament appointed several mem-bers of the Commons, including Cromwell, to meet with the army. This delegation tried to make peace with the soldiers, promising them that they would be paid.

Cromwell sought to preserve unity between Par-liament and the army, but he soon realized that this would be impossible. When he tried to describe the soldiers' deep sense of suffering to Parliament's leaders, they refused to listen to any grievances, and even demanded the immediate disbanding of Crom-well's old regiments.

If Cromwell supported Parliament in disbanding the army he would lose the influence that he had built up over the years. His troops respected him and held him in high esteem. How could he violate that trust? Moreover, Cromwell feared that without his steadying presence the army might try to carry out the extreme Leveller reforms on its own. Still, as a member of Parliament, Cromwell was sworn to carry out its orders. How could he violate this duty?

While Cromwell pondered this dilemma, events helped to force his hand. The army mutiny went forward. On June 3 the army council, consisting mainly of its chief officers, declared that the army would not disband until its grievances had been met. With the officers and the soldiers united in their demands, the army was out of Parliament's control.

On that same day the implications of the army's break from Parliament were felt when one of the junior officers, Cornet Joyce, and a body of men

The Puritans' belief that their cause was morally correct seemed ridiculous to their Cavalier opponents. Prince Charles, writing in 1650, expressed the conviction that if the parliamentarians were not stopped, ". . . the poisonous breath of this rebellion will corrupt all peoples."

asserted their newly acquired independence by seizing the king, previously under Parliament's jurisdiction. When he asked the officers by what authority they acted, Joyce pointed to the troops behind him. Now that the army had possession of the king, Parliament could do little more than sit back and watch the army negotiate the future settlement on its own.

Rumors began circulating in London that Cromwell had engineered the army mutiny and that he would soon be arrested. Rather than risk going to jail, and also because he wanted to take charge of the army at this crucial moment, Cromwell at last decided to join forces with the soldiers as soon as he learned that the army had possession of the king. In early June at Newmarket, the New Model Army was formed. Cromwell resumed his former rank of lieutenant general and his role as the army's guiding force.

Cromwell's first task was to encourage unity and

> *Is not Liberty of Conscience in Religion a Fundamental? So long as there is Liberty of Conscience for the Supreme Magistrate to exercise his conscience in erecting what Form of Church-Government he is satisfied he should set up, why should he not give the like liberty to others? Liberty of Conscience is a natural right; and he that would have it, ought to give it; having himself liberty to settle what he likes for the Public.*
> —OLIVER CROMWELL

restore discipline among the ranks. He accepted the Agitators' demand that the army would stay together until they got what they wanted. He also agreed to the regular meeting of a new army council consisting of a general, two commissioned officers, and two privates from each regiment. Cromwell was willing to listen to this council, but he made it clear he was to have final authority. Ultimate command of the army now rested with Lieutenant General Oliver Cromwell.

Cromwell rejected the Levellers' demand for the creation of an English republic, believing that the established monarchy was necessary to preserve the country's social order. He was willing to grant Charles certain concessions in return for a settlement that guaranteed religious toleration. In some respects, the army's proposals offered the king more authority than Parliament's proposals. But as usual Charles did not negotiate in good faith, and it would take the army officers several months before they realized the futility of their efforts.

In the meantime, Cromwell came under pressure from the militant Agitators to march on London. These Levellers wished to rid Parliament of the conservative leaders who had tried to disband the army. At first Cromwell urged the Agitators not to use force to remove their parliamentary opponents: ". . . that [which] we and they gain in a free way, it is better than twice so much in a forced, and will be more truly ours and our posterity's. . . ." But when anti-army riots broke out in London in July, Cromwell decided to take extreme measures. In August the army marched on the nation's capital and forced the Presbyterian leaders out of the House of Commons. The balance of power in England now belonged to the military.

Despite this changing hands of power, it was still necessary to negotiate a permanent settlement with Charles. Arguments over the conditions of this settlement had already split Parliament into two opposing factions, the radicals and the moderates. Now it was the army's turn to confront this volatile issue.

Cromwell's shrewd son-in-law, Henry Ireton, who

advised him in constitutional matters, brought forth proposals for a new written constitution. With Cromwell's support Ireton became the spokesman for the senior officers — the wealthier members of the army. Ireton's *Heads of Proposals* called for the retainment of both the king and the House of Lords, and for the men of property to be given special rights. In other words, Ireton was willing to compromise both the king and Parliament in order to ensure the rights of property holders, like himself and Cromwell. "All the main thing I speak for is because I have an eye to property," he admitted.

Ireton's *Heads of Proposals* did not come close to approaching the Levellers' radical ideas. Unsatisfied, they decided to write their own constitutional document, *The Agreement of the People*. This democratic charter, radical for its day, called for a government based upon the consent of the people. The Levellers wanted to abolish the king and the House of Lords, letting the House of Commons run the country. The Commons would be elected by all adult males, not just the rich property holders as in Ireton's and Cromwell's scheme. The Levellers were not opposed to affording rights to rich men, they simply wanted the franchise extended to the lower classes as well.

The army was clearly split over which constitution outlined the best form of government for the country. In October 1647 an historic debate took place in the town of Putney when the officers and the Agitators met to discuss the issue.

The Putney Debate is one of the most important events in English history. Cromwell served as moderator. Ireton presented the views of the officers, while various spokesmen from the rank and file gave the Leveller position. The Putney Debate is significant because it marked the first time in modern history that the principles of democracy were discussed openly.

When the debate began, Cromwell made a strong appeal for harmony. But his hopes to preserve the army's unity were shattered as rising tempers on both sides forced a confrontation. The Levellers launched into a personal attack on those officers

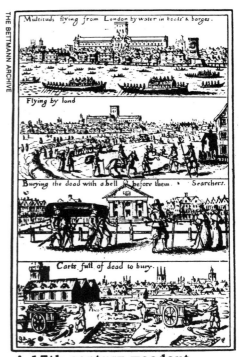

A 17th-century woodcut shows Londoners fleeing an outbreak of plague. Natural calamities contributed greatly to the uncertainty of existence in 17th-century England.

who supported Ireton's proposals. A radical army officer named Thomas Rainsborough set forth the democratic ideal: the poorest man in England deserved equal rights in politics. Ireton would not listen to these arguments, insisting that only property holders should be given political power.

Although Cromwell sided with his son-in-law, he tried to make light of the disagreements. He reminded both sides that God's majesty was much more important than forms of government. "They are dross and dung in comparison to Christ," he joked. To help cool the passions raised during the debate, and to delay resolution of the issues, Cromwell called a prayer meeting to honor God.

His real motive was to delay the proceedings in order to stop the momentum now running in favor of the radical soldiers. But his tactics did not succeed. Even after the prayer break, votes taken on specific issues, such as extending the right to vote to all Englishmen, revealed strong support for the Agitators. Cromwell then accused the Agitators of trying to divide the army. He abruptly halted the discussion, sending the Agitators back to their regiments. This forced dismissal led to grumblings and threatened counteractions among the men, but these were soon quieted by a new sensational development: The king had disappeared!

On November 11 it was learned that the king had escaped the army's custody, fleeing his quarters at Hampton Court. No one had any idea where he had gone, and some feared that if the king was no longer imprisoned he would wage another civil war. Days later however, Charles was discovered off the south coast, on the Isle of Wight, where he was once again placed in custody. By coincidence, the fortress on the Isle of Wight was commanded by one of Cromwell's many cousins.

This event played so much into Cromwell's hands that some even suspected he had engineered the whole thing in order to reunite the army in his favor. Whatever the truth, Cromwell had retained control over the army. Before the king's whereabouts were discovered, he was able to convince the army to reunite against the threat of renewed war. While most

> *The right was certainly in the king, but the exercise was yet in nobody; but contended for, as in a game at cards, without fighting, all the years between 1647 and 1648.*
>
> —THOMAS HOBBES
> 17th-century English philosopher, describing the political situation prior to the second Civil War

of the disgruntled troops agreed to follow the orders of General Fairfax rather than those of the Agitators, two radical regiments later appeared at a rendezvous without the general's approval. Sensing that the radical movement was losing its momentum, the officers moved quickly to subdue these insubordinate soldiers before they attracted further support. Cromwell himself rode into the midst of the scuffle with his sword drawn, arresting the leaders. One of the Agitators was executed as an example for the rest, and 11 others were imprisoned. Discipline was thus quickly restored.

The re-creation of army unity could not have come at a better time. Charles had succeeded in winning the Scots over to his side by promising to establish Presbyterianism as the official religion in England for a period of three years. The Scots accepted this offer and agreed to go to war against their former allies.

A 17th-century view of the Thames River in London. This great river splits London in two, and its easy navigability provided a pathway to the North Sea essential for the powerful shipping merchants of England.

S. PAULES CHURCH

Bow Church.

THAMESIS

5
Second Civil War

In December 1647 a second civil war seemed inevitable. Although the negotiations between the king and the Scots had been carried out in secret, reports circulated about a possible alliance. These rumors were given more credence when Charles completely rejected Parliament's final offer of a settlement. Members of the House of Commons, including Cromwell and Ireton, now spoke out angrily against any further negotiations with Charles. On January 3, 1648, Parliament passed a measure calling for "no further addresses." Cromwell supported this measure, arguing that the people of England could not "expect safety and government from an obstinate man whose heart God had hardened."

The implication of Cromwell's words rang clear. If Charles refused to govern the country according to Parliament's terms, a more extreme solution would have to be found. Radicals, especially in the army, believed that the only solution was to do away with the king and create a republic. Some of these Agitators called Charles "a man of blood," and demanded that he be punished.

With another war in the making, Cromwell was more determined than ever to keep the army united.

THE BETTMANN ARCHIVE

In December 1647 Charles I — portrayed here by Van Dyck — rejected Parliament's final offer of a settlement. Cromwell, enraged by the king's stubbornness, opposed further negotiations, arguing that the English people could not "expect safety and government from an obstinate man whose heart God had hardened."

BILDARCHIV, FOTO MARBURG/ART RESOURCE

Parliamentary cavalrymen in action. In the Battle of Preston, fought between August 17 and August 25, 1648, Cromwell's forces crushed a numerically superior royalist-Scottish army.

Charles I (at far end of conference table) meets with commissioners appointed by Parliament to negotiate a treaty with him, September 1648. Parliament's willingness to hold talks with the king, despite the fact that it had previously agreed not to do so, greatly angered the Levellers, who demanded that Charles be put on trial.

On December 6, 1648, Colonel Thomas Pride (center left, with sword drawn; d. 1658), an officer in the parliamentary army, ordered his troops to guard the doors to Parliament and proceeded to purge, or exclude, approximately 140 M.P.s the army considered too sympathetic toward the king. "Pride's Purge," as the event became known, set the stage for the trial of Charles I.

This would not be an easy task, for the rank and file was again on the verge of revolt. Cromwell had tried to patch up the differences between the Agitators and the officers by pleading for unity after Charles's escape in November. But his efforts had been a bit too forceful, especially the incident in which Cromwell halted a Leveller rebellion by killing one Agitator and imprisoning the rest. He was soon informed that "two thirds part of the army" threatened a mutiny if the officers did not come around to the Leveller position.

Cromwell knew that the army would have to regain the discipline and dedication that had been its trademark in the first Civil War if it hoped to defeat an expanded royalist force. Realizing that he had treated the Agitators rather roughly, he tried to win them over with some kindness. The remaining mutineers, imprisoned since November, were released and Colonel Thomas Rainsborough, a chief Leveller spokesman, was promoted to vice-admiral.

The Scots and the king had hoped to take advantage of the disunity in Parliament's army. But Cromwell countered their strategy by moving closer to the Leveller position regarding the final settlement of the kingdom. Although the sincerity of his support for Leveller reforms was questionable (". . . if we cannot bring the army to our sense, we must go to theirs," he allegedly remarked), his ploy worked. When the second Civil War finally began, the quarrel between the officers and the Agitators was over. The officers joined with the troops, pledging that upon victory Charles must be tried and executed for shedding blood in the land.

The second Civil War broke out in southern Wales in February 1648. At first the Royalist-Scottish army made a strong showing. By April the king's forces had seized two key English fortresses on the border of Scotland, and three months later a large Scottish army invaded England. The Scots arrived in stages, as another large force joined the first a month later. By August approximately 24,000 foreign soldiers had converged upon the north of England.

Cromwell had not been around during the Scots' invasion. As early as May, he had left London to put down a series of royalist uprisings in Wales. Once the turncoats had surrendered, Cromwell turned his army northward to help stop the Scottish invasion of England. His men had not been paid for months; nevertheless, their strict discipline prevented them from pillaging local farms for food and supplies. This was in contrast to the Scots, who were living off the countryside, gaining the hatred of the local population.

Bringing no more than a few thousand troops with him, Cromwell marched his army to the county of Lancashire in record time. Although ill-equipped and smaller in number than their opponents, these Ironsides were experienced soldiers and they possessed a spirit that gave them an advantage in morale. On the night of August 6, Cromwell reached a crucial decision. Rather than wait for reinforcements, he decided to attack immediately. "To fight was our business," he announced.

It is our duty, if ever the Lord brings us back again in peace, to call Charles Stuart, that man of blood, to an account for the blood he has shed, and mischief he has done to his utmost.
—resolution passed by Cromwell's army in April 1648

The Battle of Preston began on August 17, and developed into a running engagement. While most civil war battles lasted only hours, Preston resembled an extended massacre, continuing over a period of days. Cromwell's strategy was to attack the Scots from the north, thereby cutting off their escape route back to Scotland. His goal was to totally destroy the Scottish force, so that they could never regroup to fight again. The royalists provided him

with the opportunity by stretching out a long line of troops, without maintaining communication between the separate units. Cromwell concentrated on the center of the enemy line, and managed to split their army and block off their escape route at the same time. By the time the fighting ended eight days later, on August 25, the royalist army had suffered a complete and humiliating defeat.

The news of Cromwell's latest victory destroyed all

Charles I is mocked by his parliamentary guards, who are overjoyed that he has been sentenced to death, January 27, 1649. The 67 judges who condemned the king voted that "Charles Stuart, as a Tyrant, Traitor, Murderer, and Public Enemy . . . shall be put to death by the severing of his Head from his body."

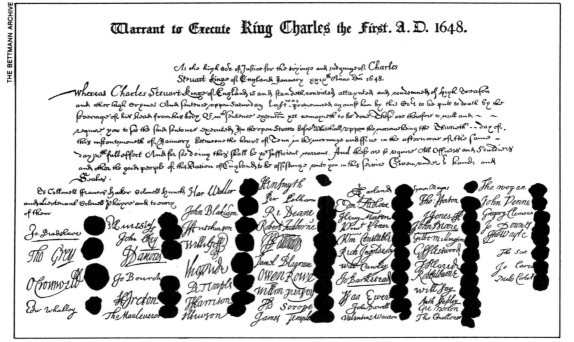

Warrant to Execute King Charles the First. A.D. 1648.

[Handwritten warrant text with signatures, largely obscured by ink blots]

Following the restoration of the Stuarts in 1660, several of those who had signed the warrant for Charles I's execution claimed that they had done so unwillingly and that Cromwell — whose signature can be seen in the column at extreme left — had taken their hands and forced them to write.

hopes the royalists might have entertained for success. Upon learning of the outcome, most royalist fortresses in England began to surrender. In Scotland, the pro-royalists were replaced by a government more favorably disposed to the English Parliament. The Battle of Preston had virtually ended the second Civil War.

Once again, the future settlement of England presented itself as the main item on the political agenda for the country. But Cromwell did not rush back to London to help plan the future peace. Instead, he crossed the northern border into Scotland to ensure that no further intervention should occur. It was almost as if Cromwell was trying to avoid participating in the peace settlement, remembering all the problems this issue had caused in the past.

With Cromwell and the main body of the army away from London, Parliament took it upon itself to arrange a settlement. The Presbyterian opponents of Cromwell, those the army had once kicked out, returned to the House of Commons and in August they helped push through a measure repealing the Vote of No Addresses the purged Parliament had passed a half year earlier. By September, the king and Parliament were conducting negotiations, despite the fact that the army had pledged to see Charles punished when the war was over. But only Parliament negotiated in earnest. Charles continued his dishonest ways, allowing the talks to drag on in order to avoid making an agreement, confident that no peace could be attained without his compliance.

The men and officers of the army did not share Parliament's eagerness to pretend that nothing had changed since the war. Most markedly, they did not care to risk the possibility of further wars brought on by an untrustworthy monarch. Having directly suffered one more time in a second and seemingly unnecessary civil war, the soldiers did not wish to forgive their king.

Charles I was beheaded on January 30, 1649. The calm dignity with which the king faced his execution made a great impression on all those who witnessed his death.

Throughout the fall of 1648, Leveller-inspired petitions were sent by various regiments to their nominal leader, General Fairfax. They contained the same message: Justice must be obtained against Charles for shedding the people's blood. There were even hints that if the officers did not join them, the rank and file would get rid of Charles on their own.

With events reaching a critical juncture, it seems odd that Cromwell chose to remain in the north, conducting a not very important siege operation. As always, reaching important decisions frequently produced anxiety in Cromwell. He preferred to pass through lengthy periods of inactivity, turning to prayer and contemplation before committing himself. It must be concluded, therefore, that Cromwell used his military duties as an excuse for not joining the events that were unfolding in London.

Since Cromwell had returned from Scotland, the mantle of leadership passed on to Ireton, his son-in-law. Ireton was not one to hesitate. As his first task, he attempted to keep the army unified. It had taken a solidly knit army to defeat the royalists, and now it would take a solidly knit army to influence politics. Ireton helped organize a new general council to work out an agreement between the moderate officers and the Leveller leaders.

The officers were willing to compromise, for they accepted the radicals' basic formulations. Chief among these was the idea that the army spoke for the whole English nation. These men were not a group of hired, mercenary soldiers, ran the argument; rather, they represented a cross-section of the country, the people of England in arms. This made them even more representative than the Parliament. With this view in mind, the army felt that it should be left to find solutions for the country's problems.

Ireton was willing to accept this concept. But if the army was to speak for the nation, he wanted the officers to be in charge and not have to share authority with the more radical enlisted men. In order to win the radicals over to his side, Ireton decided to give the impression that he would go along with most of their demands. In the middle of November 1648 he presented to Parliament a manifesto enti-

A brilliant cavalry leader of enterprise and daring, an unconventional tactician who owed nothing to early military training, a commander who created an army which was the wonder of Europe—all these laurels are willingly draped upon Cromwell's brow.
—ANTONIA FRASER
British historian

70

tled *A Remonstrance of the Army* which contained several Leveller principles. Among the proposals Ireton called for was the enacting of a constitution based upon an agreement of the people. More importantly, he proposed that the king be put on trial for attempting to establish tyranny in England.

On December 6, 1648, the army, under Ireton's direction, took their most illegal action to date. Troops commanded by Colonel Thomas Pride guarded the doors to Parliament and excluded, or purged, approximately 140 members who were considered too sympathetic to the king. Pride's Purge left only about 50 men in the House of Commons, all considered politically reliable by the army. What was left of Parliament after the purge was henceforth known as the Rump.

The stage was now set for Charles's trial, but Cromwell had not yet returned. With all of these significant developments taking place, there was an urgent need for his commanding presence. He arrived in London on the evening of Pride's Purge. Although he may have been surprised at all that had happened without his participation, he gave his complete approval to everything the army had done, including Pride's Purge.

Cromwell, however, was not yet sure what to do with the king. Perhaps just removing him from the throne and installing a replacement would suffice. To Cromwell, a republic still seemed too drastic a solution. But the Levellers and Ireton (who needed their support) pressed for a trial. Finally, giving in to his son-in-law's persuasiveness, Cromwell granted his consent. He did, however, insist that the procedure at least appear legal and respectable. Unfortunately, lawyers at that time protected people of property and very few wished to offend their aristocratic clients by lending their name to any such proceeding.

As late as December 25 Cromwell still expressed private reservations about the forthcoming trial. He did not know on what authority to prosecute the king. Parliament finally decided to create a High Court of Justice. This court would level its charge against Charles "in the name of the Commons and

> *For the people truly I desire their liberty and freedom as much as anybody whatsoever; but I must tell you that their liberty and freedom consists in having government, those laws by which their lives and goods may be most their own. It is not their having a share in the government; that is nothing appertaining to them; a subject and a sovereign are clear different things.*
> —CHARLES I
> speaking on the day of his execution

Parliament assembled and all the good people of England." Now fully convinced, Cromwell took charge over events with his usual firmness. His earlier concerns about keeping the trial legal seemed to have vanished, for when one of the moderate politicians protested to him about the illegality of trying a reigning monarch, Cromwell disdainfully replied, "We will cut off his head with the crown on it."

Cromwell's defiant statement carried a great deal of meaning. Kings of England had been removed from their throne and killed before, but never before had a king been tried while still king. It was also unheard of for such an act to be carried out in the name of the English people.

As the trial proceeded, some of the participants began having second thoughts. But Cromwell, now more determined than ever, pressured the timid to sign the warrant for execution. A few later claimed that Cromwell actually took their hands and guided their signatures. But they made these explanations only after the Stuart kings had been restored, when they were called to account for the execution and needed an excuse.

On January 30, 1649, Charles I, king of England, was brought to a scaffold in London. Had he agreed to make concessions to Parliament, Charles most likely could have saved his life, but he remained steadfast in his convictions that a king was fully responsible for his subjects and for the laws of the country. He even refused to plead for mercy during his trial. His courage in accepting his fate rather than bowing to Parliament's demands made a lasting impression on the English people.

Charles was executed by having his head severed from his body. When one of the masked executioners held up the king's head for the crowd to see, a groan arose from the people nearby. "Such a groan as I have never heard before," wrote one of the witnesses. A traditional story, probably false, recalls how Cromwell, with a cloak drawn over his face, came that night to view the departed monarch and lamented, "cruel necessity." But Cromwell was never one to regret actions taken, for he believed that God had only one course to follow.

Nor call'd the Gods with vulgar spite
To vindicate his helpless Right
But bow'd his comely Head
Down as upon a Bed.
—ANDREW MARVELL
17th-century English poet, praising Charles's resolute acceptance of execution

According to a traditional story, Cromwell viewed the king's corpse after the execution and declared that the deed had been done out of "cruel necessity."

A GENEALOGIE OF ANTI-CHRIST.

OLIVER CROMWELL *of ȳ* Fanaticks *and their* Triumphant as Head Vices, *supported by Devils.*

Anti-christ *Pontiff of* HELL. *Married*

Pride. *Daughter of Ignorance and begot*

Hereticks. Blasphemers Atheists.

Arians. Socinians Deists.

Schismaticks. Independents Anabaptists.

Tepidists. Muggletonians Libertines

Puritans. Arminians Quakers.

Brownists. Enthusiasts. Impostures

Hypocrisie. Selfconceit. Vain-glory.

Presbytery.

Ignorance, and Persecution

Fanaticism. *Married* Profaneness, *& begot seven Daughters*

Wrath. *Married to* Hatred *brought forth*

Strife. *Married to* Selfconceit *brought forth*

Sedition. *Married to* Presumption *brought forth*

Envy. *Married to* Malice, *brought forth*

Rebellion. *Married to* Treason *brought forth*

Discord. *Married to* Anarchy. *brought forth*

Civill-War. *Married to* Ruin *brought forth*

Oppression

Contention

Tumults.

Murders.

Regicides.

Confusion

Beggary.

G. Bickham Sculp.

6

The English Commonwealth

The execution of Charles I gave rise to revolutionary change. In March 1649 the monarchy and the House of Lords were formally abolished. Two months later, the House of Commons passed a law that abolished the kingdom and established the free state of the English Commonwealth.

Despite these radical changes, the Levellers were not satisfied with the way the government of the country was taking shape. For one thing, the purged House of Commons, with the trial and execution out of the way, began to grow in size as some of the more moderate members gradually resumed their places. Even two former members of the old House of Lords got themselves elected to this Rump Parliament.

The reconservatizing of Parliament was not the only thing that bothered the Levellers. They had cooperated with the army officers for the sake of army unity, only to see many of the promises made by Ireton and Cromwell unfulfilled. Now that the king had been executed, no more was heard of popular sovereignty, law reform, or expanding the vote.

THE BETTMANN ARCHIVE

In May 1649 Cromwell moved to suppress a revolt by Levellers who, not content with Parliament's abolition of the monarchy and the House of Lords, were calling for law reform and the extension of the vote. Four leading members of the movement, were summarily shot.

A 17th-century engraving entitled *A Genealogie of Anti-Christ* portrays Cromwell as the father of heretical sects responsible for numerous vices. The pejorative term "anti-Christ" was used by many different religious groups.

GIRAUDON/ART RESOURCE

Cromwell arrests a mutinous Leveller in May 1649. As a conservative landowner, Cromwell neither advocated the abolition of all economic privileges nor believed in the equality of landlord and tenant.

THE BETTMANN ARCHIVE

Although England was now a republic, the rich landlords still ruled the country and the poor had as little voice as before.

Realizing that Cromwell and Ireton had been bluffing when they claimed to have moved closer to the Levellers' position when they needed the army's support, the Levellers directed their frustrations at the two army officers. A pamphlet appropriately entitled *England's New Chains Discovered*, published in February 1649, attacked Cromwell, accusing him of seeking to rule England as despotically as the Stuart monarchs. Arrested for sedition, the Leveller leaders overheard Cromwell vehemently denouncing them: "I tell you sir, you have no other way to deal with these men but to break them, or they will break you."

Cromwell frequently served as chairman for the Council of State, a newly created executive body responsible to Parliament. But his main duties continued to be of a military nature. The new English Commonwealth possessed many enemies, both internal and external. The most pressing threat was the Irish, who had been in rebellion since 1641. An unstable Ireland could very easily serve as a base of operations for the royalists, now rallying around Charles I's eldest son, Charles II. Cromwell was chosen to command the parliamentary army sent over to put down the rebellion.

Sending troops to Ireland, however, raised some of the same issues that had arisen two years earlier, when the soldiers refused to go until their rights were secured. Still unsatisfied, three regiments scheduled to leave for Ireland threatened mutinies in May, once again refusing to obey their assignments until the liberties they had fought for had been attained. Calling for "England's freedom, soldiers' rights," they hoped to win over other regiments.

Cromwell would not stand for such a blatant breach of discipline. He used forceful action to smash this rebellion, bringing to mind his action against the Agitators who had chanted the same words in a rebellion just prior to the second Civil War. Taking his loyal troops on a forced march, Cromwell fell upon this second batch of mutineers, arresting 400 prisoners. He had four of the leaders shot for treason and the example put a restraint on the rest of the protesters. Because of his decisive response, the mutiny came to an end. Cromwell brought the soldiers back to his side by assuring all his troops that they would be paid before departing for Ireland. Three months later, in August, Cromwell finally gathered his forces and set out to pacify the Irish. This would not be one of his most honorable accomplishments.

Cromwell thought the Catholic Irish uncivilized and barbarous. As a Puritan, he believed that it was his duty in life to fulfill God's will. Directed by the anti-papacy roots of Puritanism, Cromwell came to despise the hierarchy and ritualism associated with the Catholic church. Because Cromwell justified his actions by invoking God's will, his savage repressions of the next few months have to be seen as the negative side of the Puritan's religious zeal.

Within a few weeks of arriving in Ireland, Cromwell's army captured the town of Drogheda. The entire garrison was killed. This brutal massacre went

THE BETTMANN ARCHIVE

A 17th-century engraving shows Irish men and women in traditional dress. Cromwell and his compatriots felt great contempt toward the Irish. Historian Christopher Hill writes that even those Englishmen "who believed passionately in liberty and human dignity . . . all shared the view that the Irish were culturally so inferior that their subordination was natural and necessary."

Irish soldiers and their families evacuate Limerick following that city's capture in 1651 by parliamentary troops led by Henry Ireton. Ireton succeeded Cromwell as commander in chief in Ireland in April 1650, when Cromwell returned to London to prepare for war with the Scots, who had proclaimed Charles II king.

beyond anything done in any previous battle of the Civil War. Cromwell, however, felt justified: "I am persuaded that this is a righteous judgment of God upon these barbarous wretches, who have imbrued their hands in so much innocent blood."

Exactly one month after the Drogheda massacre, in October 1649, a similar fate befell the town of Wexford. Cromwell's usually well-disciplined soldiers were allowed to run wild through the conquered town. Between 1,500 and 2,000 Irish soldiers, civilians, and priests were murdered in the slaughter.

The reign of terror seemed to work, for several other Irish fortresses surrendered soon afterwards without resistance. By the time Cromwell moved his army into winter quarters, most of the Irish coast had been won over to English control. As spring 1650 arrived, Parliament's forces moved inland to continue the siege warfare. In April, when Cromwell received an emergency summons to return home to England, only a few Irish garrisons remained to be conquered. In his absence Henry Ireton served as commander in chief. But Ireton did not survive long enough to witness final victory in Ireland. Cromwell's son-in-law died of fever in November 1651. A half year later the last resisting town, Galway, sur-

rendered. Ireland was now completely under English domination.

Cromwellian rule in Ireland continued the traditional English policy of suppressing the Catholics and trying to establish Protestantism. But under Cromwell the repressive measures became much more severe. Priests and officers were either imprisoned or sent into exile, although civilians were generally spared. Despite temporary success, these drastic policies eventually backfired, as Ireland continued to cling to its Roman Catholicism. The intractable Irish problems in English history established deep roots during this period.

Cromwell had been summoned back to England because of the threat of a new war with Scotland. By the time he returned in May 1650 the Scots had already proclaimed the son of Charles I the new king of England and Ireland, as well as Scotland. When Scotland undertook to restore Charles II to his father's vacant throne, Cromwell clamored for war: ". . . a just and necessary defence of ourselves, for preservation of those rights and liberties which Divine Providence hath, through the expense of so much blood and treasure, given us. . . ."

On June 26, 1650, Parliament appointed Cromwell commander in chief of all the forces of the Commonwealth. By the end of July an English army once again entered Scotland. The early stages of this campaign proved extremely frustrating because the Scots refused to fight. They avoided the English army, hoping that disease and shortages would eventually cripple the enemy. Even an unopposed bombardment of their capital, Edinburgh, failed to lure the Scots into battle. As the English army tried desperately to draw the Scots into a major engagement, soldiers began to die from disease. Having come into the country with 16,000 men, within a month the English were down to 11,000. This is exactly what the Scots were counting on.

Early in September 1650 the Scottish generals decided it was time to alter their strategy. Now outnumbering the English approximately two to one, they were able to outmaneuver them as well. Occupying a hill overlooking the city of Dunbar, the

THE BETTMANN ARCHIVE

An Irish cartoon shows a parliamentary soldier laden with plunder. Cromwell's determination to subdue the Irish as quickly as possible led him to proceed against them with singular brutality: at Wexford, in October 1649, his troops slaughtered between 1,500 and 2,000 Irish soldiers and civilians.

Scots closed off the line of escape for the English, who were hemmed in by the hills and the sea behind them. With victory seemingly assured, the Scots looked forward to overrunning England. Scottish General Leslie confidently gave the signal for his men to descend, attacking the English from the advantage of their high position.

The sight of the Scottish army charging down the hill did not faze Cromwell in the least. For him, any opportunity to engage in battle represented a chance for victory. He attributed this turn of fortune to God's intervention. "God is delivering them into our hands, they are coming down to us!" he cried.

Leslie's troops were overconfident. They failed to conduct their descent in an orderly fashion. Cromwell's experienced military eye observed that despite their large numbers, the Scots had cramped themselves against the hill, giving them little room to maneuver. Even worse, there were large gaps in their line of march. On September 3, just before daybreak, Cromwell moved a strong body of horse and foot soldiers across a ravine separating the two armies. Pretending to attack on the Scots' left flank, he then threw most of his men against the center and right of the enemy. At a critical point, Cromwell's own regiment fell upon an exposed flank of Scottish cavalry. Pinned against the hill and the ravine, the Scottish infantry was completely overwhelmed. Three thousand Scots fell in battle and ten thousand were taken prisoner. Originally outpositioned and with many fewer soldiers, the victory at Dunbar had to be considered one of Cromwell's greatest.

The impressive victory at Dunbar, however, did not end the war. English troops now occupied southern Scotland, including Edinburgh, but a Scottish army still survived. Displaying much more charity towards fellow Protestants than he had shown to the Irish, Cromwell expressed his "longing to have avoided blood in this business." He even tried to preach toleration to the rigid Presbyterian fathers in Edinburgh. "I beseech you in the bowels of Christ, think it possible you may be mistaken," he urged. All to no avail.

Cromwell and his men sing a psalm before battle with the Scots at Dunbar, September 1650. The Scottish threat to the Commonwealth — the free English state established by Parliament in May 1649 — was finally neutralized when Cromwell crushed Charles II's combined royalist-Scottish army at the Battle of Worcester on September 3, 1651.

Once more the Scottish army avoided battle. And again the extreme cold of the northern winter took its toll on the English. Cromwell, beginning to feel the burdens of war, wrote to his wife, "I grow an old man, and feel the infirmities of age marvellously stealing upon me." In February 1651 Cromwell caught a fever, brought on by exposure to the inclement weather. It was his most serious affliction to date.

Parliament sent two of the best doctors in England to treat him. Nevertheless, Cromwell had three relapses. The doctors advised him to return home for a rest and a change of air, but he refused. Not until June did he sufficiently recover to resume the war with the Scots.

The Scottish tactics of delay and avoidance had not changed over time; their army was as elusive as ever. During his illness Cromwell had plenty of time to consider strategy. He decided to take a calculated risk in order to bring the war to a conclusion. Taking his army further north into Scotland, he left the roads to England unprotected, exposed to an easy invasion.

The young Charles II took the bait. By August 5 the Scottish army crossed over the border to invade England. On the very next day, having arrived on English soil, Charles had himself crowned king of England. He issued a call for the English people to join him against Parliament and its army. But the response of a country longing for peace, after years of sacrifice, was rather cool. This unenthusiastic reaction should have warned the Scots about the impossibility of gaining any support in a foreign land. It did not matter that they came in the name of the king. A Scottish invasion of their country set off patriotic feelings in the people of England.

Before long the Scots found themselves trapped in the city of Worcester, surrounded by three separate parliamentary armies led by Cromwell. On September 3, exactly one year after the great victory at Dunbar, the deciding battle of this war took place. Worcester would prove to be the last battle Cromwell would ever fight, but it revealed once more his mastery as a commander. His men's conduct was dis-

Cromwell's foreign enterprises though full of intrepidity were pernicious to national interest and seemed more the result of impetuous fury of narrow prejudices, than of cool foresight and deliberations.
—DAVID HUME
18th-century Scottish
philosopher and historian

ciplined and well coordinated, and he himself again displayed exemplary personal courage. One of his troops later wrote: "My Lord General did exceedingly hazard himself riding up and down in the midst of battle."

There could be little doubt about the battle's outcome. The royalist army was decimated. Not a single Scottish regiment survived, and half the Scottish nobility was taken prisoner. Scotland would lose its independence for the rest of the decade. Miraculously, the king managed to escape. After a series of adventures (traveling in disguise and hiding in a hollowed oak tree) Charles II found a ship to take him across the English Channel to France. He would not return for another nine years.

The conquering Cromwell triumphantly returned to London. Parliament, delighted with his crushing defeat of the royalist forces, voted him £4,000 a year for life and presented him with the royal estate at Hampton Court. Without a doubt, Cromwell had now become the most important individual in England. Commander of the army and member of Parliament, Cromwell was also the leader of the Council of State, the executive body created in 1649. In elections to the council in 1651 and 1652, he always was selected first. Rumors began to circulate that Cromwell would soon make himself king.

But ambition does not seem to have been a Cromwellian vice. He continued to behave with humility, attributing his own success to the will of God. Regarding his acquisition of power as a burden, he was also aware of his personal limitations ("my weaknesses, my inordinate passions, my unskillfulness, and every way unfitness to my work," he pointed out). But he knew that for some reason God wanted him to serve. Now placed into a key position in the country, he had no choice but to continue to exercise leadership.

One of the problems facing Cromwell was the instability of the present government. More permanent institutions definitely were needed. The Rump Parliament, which had grown in size after Charles I's execution, became increasingly discreditable. Its members were seen as opportunistic and without

Charles II, disguised as an ordinary citizen and accompanied by his companion, Jane Lane, evades capture by parliamentary troops following his army's defeat at the Battle of Worcester.

principle. Conservative in politics, they refused to reform the laws or to get rid of the established church. When a call for fresh elections for a new Parliament was heard throughout the land, the Rump seemed to do everything possible to avoid the issue.

More than anything else, the Rump wanted to get rid of the army, which was still out of its control. With the threat from the royalists now totally removed, the army should have been dissolved. But the army had come to regard itself as the conscience of the English revolution. If any significant reforms were to be carried out in both church and state, Parliament had to be pressured. Because this pressure could only come from the military, none of the leaders of the New Model Army wished to carry out the demobilization that Parliament desired.

The peculiar nature of Cromwell's role left him caught in the middle, straddling more than one position. He wanted to relieve the heavy burden of taxation, which a large army required for support. But he feared that this present Parliament might undermine the whole cause for which all the blood had been shed in the Civil War. A dedicated and reform-minded Parliament that both Cromwell and the army could trust would be the solution. But how could one be created?

In December 1651 Cromwell arranged a meeting between the leading members of the Rump and the chief officers in the army. With the old king gone and his son defeated, he argued, they needed to achieve a permanent settlement. But no agreement could be reached. Cromwell asked the Rump to put an early end to its sessions, so that fresh elections would be held. He hoped a newly elected Parliament would play the key role in establishing a permanent government. But the best the Rump politicians were willing to do was to set a date three years in the future for such an event.

This Parliament evidently had no desire to relinquish its position. Cromwell did not quite know how to handle the situation. As usual, he decided to wait, hoping that a remedy would present itself.

Some of the pressure for an immediate decision

Cromwell was of a sanguine complexion, naturally of such a vivacity, hilarity and alacrity as another man is when he hath drunken a cup too much.
—RICHARD BAXTER
17th-century Puritan writer

was removed when a naval war broke out between England and Holland when the English tried to weaken the Dutch position in world trade. Despite the fact that both countries were Protestant, commercial rivalries dictated foreign policy in this instance. Although Cromwell appeared to believe that it was the Dutch who initiated the conflict, he opposed the war on religious grounds.

As the war dragged on, many began to criticize Parliament for supporting the war. The army, in particular, annoyed at the navy's diversion of funds, wanted action taken. In August 1652 a council of officers presented Cromwell with a resolution, asking for immediate dissolution of the Rump, and for the election of a new, more representative assembly. Cromwell, however, used his influence to tone down these demands. When the army's petition finally reached Parliament, it merely requested certain governmental reforms and complained about the failure to adequately pay the troops. Nothing was mentioned about new elections.

Nevertheless, army dissatisfaction could not be permanently stifled, even by Cromwell. Other generals began to gain support. Particularly popular were Major Generals John Lambert and Thomas Harrison. Lambert pushed for more initiatives from the army, and Harrison favored bringing the entire country along the paths of Christian righteousness.

Throughout the winter of 1652–53 the pressure on Cromwell to take more drastic action continued to grow. When the army learned that conservative parliamentary lawyers had tried to convince Cromwell to accept a new monarch, the soldiers became even more agitated. If Cromwell did not find a solution quickly, events might pass completely out of his control.

The crisis reached its peak on April 19, 1653. It centered on the issue of new elections. Cromwell finally decided that a new Parliament committed to reforms should replace the present body. But on the following day he learned that Parliament had pushed through a measure that would allow Parliament to supervise and control the election of its successors. Cromwell could take no more of this stubborn Parliament.

Dressed as an ordinary civilian, "in plain black clothes," Cromwell rushed over to the House of Parliament, where the speaker was preparing to place the new bill to a vote. Cromwell turned to General Harrison and whispered, "This is the time I must do it." He stood up and calmly began to address the House.

When he started to list the glaring faults of this Parliament, his calm tone turned into fervent passion. He pointed out individual members who were corrupt and fraudulent. "Perhaps you think that this is not parliamentary language," he cried, "I confess it is not." When members of Parliament began to protest, Cromwell bluntly answered, "You are no Parliament, I say you are no Parliament, I will put an end to your sitting." He then ordered Harrison to bring in 25 musketeers, who had been waiting in the lobby.

The soldiers forced the speaker from his chair, throwing him and the rest of the members out of the building. Cromwell turned to them once more: "It is you that have forced me to do this, for I have sought the Lord night and day, that he would rather slay me than put me upon doing of this work."

The Long Parliament, which Cromwell had joined as a member from Cambridge some 13 years before, was now brought to a close. Later that day, Cromwell also dismissed the Council of State. The Commonwealth thus ended and a new phase of English history was about to begin.

A 17th-century illustration shows Cromwell (foreground, third from left) dismissing Parliament, April 19, 1653. The dismissal signaled the end of the English Commonwealth and paved the way for the return of the Protectorate.

7

The Protectorate

Very few people mourned the passing of Parliament. "There was not so much as the barking of a dog or any other general and visible repining of it," Cromwell observed. True, but what would take its place? Now lacking a Parliament as well as a king, the structure of the government was even more precarious than before. Cromwell had no idea what to do, for no plans had been made in advance of his sudden dissolution of the Long Parliament. He could have set up a military dictatorship, with himself in command, but Cromwell did not want such a drastic solution. Instead, he wanted to establish institutions that would survive without him.

Respecting Cromwell's desire for legality and for parliamentary rule, the army officers supported the creation of a nominated Parliament that would serve as "supreme authority." Cromwell and the officers agreed that this new body would consist only of members "fearing God and of approved fidelity and honesty," reflecting the power of the religious faction in the army.

The 140 members of this innovative Parliament were selected by Cromwell, Harrison (leader of the religious extremists in the army) and churches

Cromwell's Great Seal shows the Lord Protector on horseback. Cromwell's opposition to egalitarian Puritanism became increasingly pronounced during the first months of the Protectorate. To Parliament he declared: "We would keep up the nobility and the gentry."

The Great Seal of the English Commonwealth, struck in 1651 ("in the third year of freedom by God's blessing restored," according to the legend inscribed around its edge), depicts the House of Commons during a debate.

throughout the country. As a result, many of those selected adhered to the sect, then quite prominent, known as the Fifth Monarchists. These zealots believed in the imminent second coming of Christ, which would establish the eternal kingdom of God.

The somewhat fanatical religious nature of this new assembly lent itself to ridicule. The nickname, "Barebones Parliament," arose because one of its members was known as "Praise God Barbon." He was a leather merchant from London who, like some of his fellow members, was a lay preacher. When Cromwell summoned the new Parliament to meet in July 1653, he soon became dismayed with the whole enterprise. He would later describe the Barebones Parliament as "a story of my own folly."

The Barebones was perceived to be a group of religious fanatics by Cromwell and the rest of the country because of their radical reform proposals. Some of these proposals — abolishing executions of first-time pickpockets, no longer pressing to death accused persons who refused to plead, and pardoning debtors who were bankrupt — are not as shocking now as they were in the 17th century. The proposal that caused the most alarm was the call for religious practices in England to be made totally independent of the state, with each individual parish free to do whatever it wished. At that time, the idea of unsupervised individual churches was considered dangerous. Cromwell began to complain that he was "more troubled now with the fool, than before with the knave."

When Cromwell refused to support their radical program, the more extreme members of the Barebones began to denounce him as "the man of sin, the old dragon and many other scriptured ill names." Even the army became a target for these members, who labeled the soldiers "pensioners of Babylon." Some Barebones radicals intended to use the forum of Parliament to proclaim new heavens, and to prepare for the second coming. Self-styled holy men would come into Parliament with their Bibles in hand, interrupting the session to describe "an extraordinary call directly to them from Christ."

By December 1653 the conservative members of

THE BETTMANN ARCHIVE

A 17th-century engraving shows members of the minority Protestant sect known as the Society of Friends (or Quakers) conducting a meeting. As Lord Protector, Cromwell urged official toleration of such sects and secured the release of a number of Quakers who had been imprisoned for their beliefs.

this unique assemblage could not take any more of these strange proceedings. Various legislative proposals of a practical nature had come to a standstill, and the ones that the radicals were trying to push through made the conservatives fear for their property. On the 12th, a group of these moderates marched out of a session and voluntarily resigned their authority, placing it in Cromwell's hands. A hard core group of about 30 remained in Parliament until a troop of soldiers arrived and requested that they leave. The colonel in charge is reported to have asked them what they were doing. "We are seeking the Lord," one replied. "Then you must go elsewhere," the soldier retorted, "for to our knowledge he hasn't been seen here for years." Thus ended the short life of the Barebones Parliament.

Cromwell had not participated in the scheme that led to the termination of the Barebones Parliament. Although quite disillusioned with its fanatical nature, he did not wish to be party to a second forcible expulsion of a parliament. But he was relieved that the Barebones had been dissolved, and set out to find a workable alternative. Once again, Cromwell was in a position to assume dictatorial power. Yet he refused any offer to be made king. It was always his goal to find a way for England to be governed representatively. Not accidentally, a new plan for a settlement had just been drawn up and presented to him.

The maneuver that ended the Barebones Parliament had been engineered by army officers led by General Lambert. While the wild deliberations of the Barebones assembly had been going on, he and other discontented officers had drawn up a new written constitution, the *Instrument of Government*. As soon as Cromwell had received back the authority from the moderates, a delegation of officers requested him to accept the *Instruments*, their proposal for a new form of government.

The proposal called for Cromwell to take over executive authority with the title of "Lord Protector," since he refused to be made king. To avoid what he believed to be inevitable "blood and confusion" if the country remained in such an unstable state,

> *You are as like the forming of God as ever people were. . . . You are at the edge of promises and prophesies.*
> —OLIVER CROMWELL
> addressing the Barebones
> Parliament, in July 1653

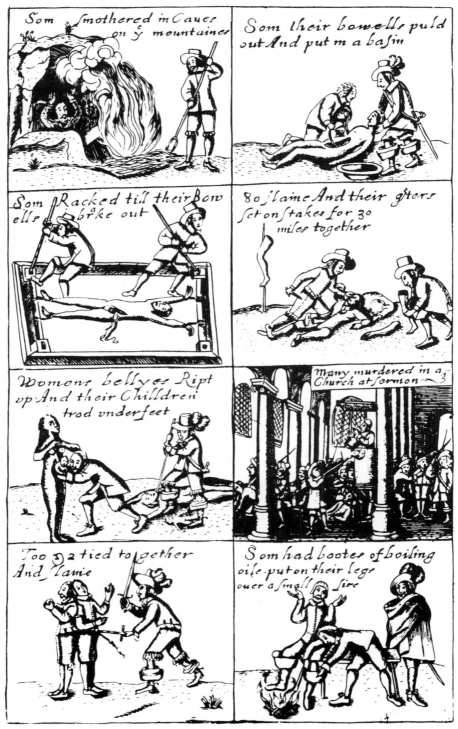

These illustrations show dissenters being tortured by the Inquisition, the religious tribunal used by the Catholic church to punish heresy.

Cromwell finally agreed. On December 16, 1653, dressed not as a general, but in civilian clothes with a plain black coat, Cromwell was solemnly installed in this majestic office.

The new government, called the Protectorate, stands out as a unique arrangement in English history. It was the first time that the country would be organized under a written constitution. "His highness, Lord Protector" was specifically described as holding an elected office, not a hereditary one. The Protector would share power with a council of state and also an elected parliament. The Council of State had the authority to elect Cromwell's successor, and it participated in decisions connected with foreign and domestic affairs. Cromwell acknowledged his legal limitations, saying that he was "a child in swaddling clothes."

The *Instrument of Government*, despite its legal trappings, helped disguise the fact that the government in England belonged to the military. The document put a great deal of power in the hands of the Council, which happened to be controlled by the army officers. For nine months before the first Protectorate Parliament was scheduled to meet, Cromwell and the Council ran the country. In so doing they dismissed radicals from the Council, in an effort to establish a professional, rather than ideological government.

A constructive first step was to attain peace with their Protestant enemy, Holland. In April 1654 the Dutch finally agreed to a treaty. Moreover, Holland promised to stop helping the English royalists. Treaties of a commercial nature with both Sweden and Denmark followed shortly afterwards. English trade was now more secure than ever. The English fleet, under the command of Admiral Robert Blake, had become a major force from the Baltic Sea to the Mediterranean Sea. At one point, it had even subdued the Algerian pirates, who had been harassing trading ships for years. These accomplishments in foreign affairs demonstrated that Cromwell recognized the importance of trade to the well-being of England. This is not surprising, for the Calvinistic roots of his Puritanism sanctified the virtues of

> *I have been desired and advised as well by several Persons of Interest and Fidelity in this Commonwealth, as the Officers of the Army, to take upon me the Protection and Government of these Nations.*
> —OLIVER CROMWELL
> taking oath as Lord Protector

thrift and diligence in business. By encouraging commercial wealth, Cromwell added to the greatness of England.

Cromwell contributed greatly to the growth of the English educational system. "No commonwealth could flourish without learning," he once remarked. He also sought to preserve the country's historical cathedrals and monuments, demonstrating his appreciation for art and culture.

Bringing the diverse political and religious factions in England back together was one of Cromwell's major concerns. He tried to convince the royalists to come over to his side, but without much success. He was much more successful in uniting the various religious sects. A Puritan church had been informally established that permitted a wide range of beliefs. The only requirement for membership was the acceptance of the chief principles of Christianity.

For the most part, Anglicans and Catholics who leaned towards allegiance with the king were excluded from the liberty of worship. But these policies were not strictly enforced. Anglicans were allowed to hold their own services, except on those few occasions when royalist plots were discovered. Even English Catholics could practice their religion privately, without too much interference from the government. Ireland, however, remained an area where repression of Catholics continued.

Relatively speaking, Cromwell was far more tolerant than most of his contemporaries. As Lord Protector he tried to end all governmental persecution of minority Protestant groups. The Society of Friends (Quakers), a fringe sect, benefited from this rule; in fact, many of them were released from prison. Another example of unusual toleration for his time had to do with the Jews. Overcoming resistance from his own council, Cromwell succeeded in allowing Jews to return to a country that had expelled them almost four centuries earlier. Cromwell furthered religious freedom at a time when few others in England or elsewhere shared his liberal views.

One area where a Puritan approach tended to be

> *Weeds and nettles, briars and thorns, have thriven under your shadow, dissettlement and division, discontentment and dissatisfaction, together with real dangers to the whole.*
> —OLIVER CROMWELL
> dissolving the first
> Protectorate Parliament

restrictive was in Parliament's passing of legislation that affected personal behavior. The Protectorate Parliament called for a stricter observance of the Sabbath. Closings of inns and taverns on Sundays became the rule. Punishments for swearing, gambling and drunkenness were made more severe, and adultery became a capital offense. In truth, however, very few of these laws were enforced. Juries refused to convict persons for some of the more ridiculous restrictions on individual rights.

Cromwell enjoyed sports and roughhousing with his men. He drank wine and beer in moderation, and opposed those prudes who wanted to prohibit all alcoholic beverages in England. He regarded such measures as violations of personal liberty. He once argued that it was not fair to "keep wine out of the country lest man should get drunk."

Even in regard to his own position as Lord Protector, Cromwell conducted himself with humility. With all his great accomplishments, he maintained a sense of modesty. Never a man of extravagant tastes, he disliked luxury and ostentation.

A 17th-century lithograph shows a Dutch trading fleet assembling prior to departing for the East Indies. The victory gained by the Protectorate in the Anglo-Dutch War of 1652—54 led to the eclipse of Dutch commercial supremacy and warned other European maritime powers that England was a force with which to be reckoned.

The most difficult task confronting Cromwell was the handling of Parliament. His rule would not be legitimate until Parliament approved his new authority. He desperately wanted to establish a working agreement with Parliament that would lead to a permanent legal settlement, a goal he had been aiming at for years. Unfortunately, it would be one goal that he never would obtain, and his failure to do so would eventually lead to the restoration of the Stuart monarchy.

The difficulty was due to the incompatibility of aims. Parliament, on the one hand, wished to reduce the size of the army, thereby reducing the burden of taxes and also making Parliament supreme in the land. This had been one of the main goals of the Civil War. But Cromwell and his generals still did not trust Parliament to carry out the program outlined in the *Instrument of Government*. This program called for establishing a permanent republic, continuing religious toleration, and reforming the laws of the land to provide greater equality.

The first Protectorate Parliament of 1654 met on an historic day, September 3, the anniversary of the great military victories of Dunbar and Worcester. In his long and powerful speech, Cromwell asked the parliamentary members to join him in the essential task of "healing and settling" by adhering to the articles outlined in the *Instrument of Government*. In other words, Parliament's job was merely to help the Protector and the Council run the country by passing laws and raising taxes.

But Parliament was not content with the role of a quiet helper. True, Cromwell was readily accepted as head of state, but members refused to accept the new constitution, arguing that it gave the military too much power. From the very beginning of its sessions Parliament expressed dissent. Because no further work could be accomplished until the issue of the constitution was settled, Cromwell was willing to compromise. In return for Parliament's promise to maintain fundamental principles, he would make some alterations in the constitution.

Four basic negotiating points were raised: How would government be divided between the Protector and Parliament? How was control over the military to be divided? What limitation was to be set on the time Parliament was to sit? And to what extent was liberty of conscience to be guaranteed?

To ease discussion, 100 of the most stubborn members of Parliament withdrew. Even so, no agreement could be reached. The two most difficult issues to settle had to do with religious toleration and control over the army. Cromwell refused to budge on either of these.

The need for a permanent settlement was brought home to Cromwell more forcefully than ever when two events occurring in the fall of 1654 reminded him of his own mortality. In September he was thrown from his horse, with his foot still caught in a stirrup, and his pistol went off, barely missing

In this 1658 Dutch cartoon deriding Cromwell as "The Horrible Tail-Man," Dutch merchants (at left) attempt to sever the Lord Protector's tail (which is filled with money) as Cromwell's advisers look on.

him. Luckily he suffered only a leg injury, but it put him out of action for weeks. Then in November, while still recuperating, he experienced the death of his beloved mother. The two had always been very close, and Cromwell felt the loss deeply.

As winter arrived, Parliament had yet to pass a single piece of legislation. Cromwell realized that he would never be able to reach an agreement with Parliament. Reluctantly and bitterly, Cromwell decided to break the stalemate by closing Parliament's doors forever. He told the members, "It is not for the profit of these nations, nor fit for the common and public good for you to continue here any longer."

As Cromwell tried to come up with something to take Parliament's place as the country's legislative body, the need for a permanent solution became more pressing. England was developing into an extremely unstable land.

Rumors of conspiracy circulated widely. In Scotland, a plot to overthrow the English government was discovered before it got started. In England, General Harrison, disappointed by the termination of the Barebones Parliament, threatened violent actions (as a preventative measure Harrison was imprisoned). Also in England, the Levellers planned to incite the soldiers into rebellion. Leveller leader John Wildman was arrested while writing a "Declaration of the free and well-affected people . . . in arms against the tyrant, Oliver Cromwell." Finally, a Cavalier plot to take over the government was quelled when several royalist agents were seized.

One actual uprising did break out in the west, where royalist sentiments had always been strong. Led by Colonel John Penruddock, 400 men proclaimed Charles II king, and started to march on Cromwell, hoping to gain further support. But a body of Ironsides easily overtook the rebels, promptly executing their leaders.

With so many plotting against him, Cromwell had to look for a drastic remedy. He had reduced the number of soldiers in the spring of 1655 in order to cut expenses, but now he completely reversed the process. Not only did he expand the army, but he also imposed military rule throughout the country. England was divided into 11 separate districts, each under the command of a major general. Each general was responsible for maintaining order in his assigned district. To fund this entire operation, Cromwell placed a 10 percent tax on the income of ex-royalists, as a sort of penalty tax.

Although the rule of the generals served its purpose by providing a firmer measure of internal security, it turned out to be the most unpopular policy ever enacted by Cromwell. Not surprisingly, the English did not take too readily to military control. As criticism rose, Cromwell assumed an even more authoritarian position: "If there be any man that hath a face looking averse to this, I dare pronounce him to be a man against the interest of England."

As the major generals were given extensive powers in running local government, they encountered opposition from the rich landowners. For most of its history, England had been governed with the cooperation of the rural upper classes. Now the country was being directed by the central authorities in London, without any local input. Cromwell, who always strove to establish a tolerant and representative government, had now created one of the most repressive despotisms England would ever experience. His only justification for the rule of generals was that it provided national security, but Cromwell's stated defense, in truth, did not even satisfy himself.

As the Protector's domestic policies continued to escape a final and satisfactory resolution, he demonstrated greater success in the field of foreign affairs. After concluding peace with the Dutch, Cromwell wished to improve relations with France as well. He negotiated a commercial treaty with the French that soon led to a close military alliance as well. An immediate benefit was the acquisition of the channel seaport city of Dunkirk, providing England with an important bridgehead on the European continent. Another beneficial aspect of his new foreign policy was an alliance formed with Portugal, which provided a large market for English goods.

Even more ambitious was Cromwell's plan to chal-

During a great part of the eighteenth century most Tories hated Cromwell because he overthrew the monarchy, most Whigs because he overthrew Parliament. More recently, liberals have seen in him their champion, and all revolutionists have apotheosized the first great representative of their school; while on the other side, their opponents have hailed the dictator who put down anarchy.
—W.C. ABBOTT
British historian

lenge Spain's domination of trade in the West Indies. The attempt to seize Hispaniola (now Haiti and the Dominican Republic) met with disastrous results, but an English fleet did manage to take over the island of Jamaica, which remained in British hands until 1962. The Protector had also hoped to eliminate some of his government's financial burdens by seizing valuable Spanish treasure ships returning from the New World. This scheme was not entirely successful. In 1656 an English captain did confiscate some £7,000 worth of silver, but a Spanish ship carrying about three times that amount sank in the Atlantic Ocean, its booty lost forever.

The most important aspect of Cromwell's foreign policy was the creation of England as a major world power, reminiscent of the days of Cromwell's beloved Queen Elizabeth. From the Caribbean to the Mediterranean seas, the English navy had in a very short time become a force to be respected. Yet the new important role England played throughout the world did little to strengthen support for the Protectorate at home.

A need remained for regular sources of income to finance the large military force that Cromwell used to enforce order. Like his predecessor, Charles I, Cromwell found that he could not finance his government without Parliament's help except by resorting to arbitrary taxation. Some of Cromwell's income came from the tariffs he levied on trade, drawing opposition from merchants. A London businessman named George Cory became so fed up with the taxes he had to pay for imported silk that he refused to pay. When he was brought to trial, Cory's lawyers questioned the validity of taxes that had not been approved by Parliament, calling into question the legitimacy of the government itself. Raising such constitutional issues got those lawyers quickly sent to the Tower of London. And the judge in the case, who sympathized with their arguments, lost his position. Cromwell had already attempted to prohibit criticisms of the Protectorate by putting an end to the free press and appointing a commissioner to censor all pamphlets and newspapers. But censorship and imprisonment did not silence his critics. Word spread that the Cromwellian government was as tyrannical as those of the Stuart kings.

The growing tendency of the Protectorate to follow in the paths of its predecessors became an embarrassment. A radical army officer, Edmund Ludlow, warned Cromwell against "a reestablishment of that which we all engaged against, and had with a great expense of blood and treasure abolished." But while Cromwell agreed with Ludlow that there was a need for a government by consent, he feared for England's future. The problem he could not solve was how to arrange a representative government that would not fall into the hands of royalists, who would use bribery to get back into power.

A royalist cartoon portrays Cromwell as the architect of anarchy: under his direction a mob cuts down "The Royal Oake of Brittayne," from whose branches hang symbols of royalty and the Magna Charta (a document guaranteeing the English certain civil and political liberties).

8

Last Years

Compounding Cromwell's dilemma was his realization that time was running out on him. In the winter of 1655–56, now approaching 57 years of age, his health began to deteriorate. He suffered from gout, stones, and a boil on his chest that took a long time to heal. Clearly the strain of all the years of being an active soldier, combined with the burden of high office, began to weaken his once sturdy physical condition.

Nevertheless, the responsibilities of governing England continued. An open war with Spain intensified during the early part of 1656. Supplies were needed, and Cromwell decided that these should be obtained legally, through a parliamentary vote. Cromwell did not have to summon a new assembly until 1657, under the terms of the *Instrument of Government*, but his major generals convinced him that elections for a new Parliament, under their supervision, would bring in "friendly" representation. The elections were held in the summer, but the results were far different than had been predicted.

Despite the generals' efforts, a large number of opposition candidates succeeded in getting elected. To offset the overabundance of hostile critics, the

THE BETTMANN ARCHIVE

Cromwell's daughter Elizabeth (1629–58) enjoyed an excellent relationship with her father, who showed her much love and affection, and greatly respected her intellectual abilities, which were considerable.

An angry Cromwell broods over the criticism to which he was subjected in a Leveller pamphlet entitled *Killing No Murder* (a copy of which can be seen at his feet) in 1657. The pamphlet branded Cromwell a tyrant and advocated his assassination.

Council of State decided to inspect the credentials of all new members. Quite arbitrarily, about 100 and possibly more were excluded right from the start. To Cromwell's surprise, the remaining members proved to be no more compliant than the excluded ones. Once again, the Protector faced a defiant Parliament.

When the session began, however, the members took the time to praise Cromwell, demonstrating their respect for him as the Lord Protector. But they also made it clear that they strongly opposed the illegal taxes raised during the previous 18 months of military rule. No further financial grants would be approved until the military rule was ended. In January 1657 this second Protectorate Parliament defeated a tax necessary for the continuation of military government, and the experiment of ruling a country by armed men came to a halt. To a large extent, the generals' failure to elect a cooperative Parliament accounted for their own defeat. But the truth remains that the military government had few civilian supporters in England. In fact, this experiment was so discredited that never again would any English government resort to such a drastic remedy. A century or so after Cromwell, when the British used a standing army of redcoats to discipline

Elizabeth Cromwell entreats her father to refuse the crown, offered by Parliament, in 1657. Alarmed by an assassination attempt on the Lord Protector, Parliament wanted to ensure England's political stability by reverting to monarchy.

the American colonies, the attempt again backfired.

One serious area of disagreement between Cromwell and this Parliament had to do with the Protector's commitment to religious freedom. The growth of the Society of Friends (Quakers) disturbed the moderate property holders, especially because the Quakers showed little respect for the social ranking of English society. These moderates used an incident involving Quaker leader James Naylor to discredit Cromwell's policy of liberty of religion.

Naylor, a somewhat unstable individual, rode into the city of Bristol on a donkey, deliberately imitating Christ's entry into Jerusalem on Palm Sunday. For this sacrilegious deed, he was arraigned before Parliament, whose members took turns suggesting horrendous punishments for him.

At this point Cromwell personally intervened. In a letter sent to Parliament, he denied having any sympathy for Naylor. But he suggested that only the courts of the land could try him, not Parliament. Although the sentence would eventually call for Naylor to be severely punished by flogging, branding, and being indefinitely imprisoned, Cromwell's intervention undoubtedly saved his life.

The case of James Naylor raised the issue of how power was to be divided between Parliament and the Protector. And once the elimination of the major generals' political role took place, a reordering of the government became essential. In the middle of these discussions, a new plot to assassinate Cromwell was

Cromwell refuses Parliament's request that he become king, May 1657. Cromwell's decision was influenced by the fact that many of his old military colleagues were bitterly opposed to the idea. Colonel Pride, who had purged Parliament of royalist sympathizers in 1648, is reported to have said that he would have shot Cromwell had he accepted the kingship.

On December 17, 1656, Quaker leader James Naylor (1617–60), found guilty of blasphemy by Parliament, was first flogged, then had his tongue burned through with a hot iron, and, finally, had his forehead branded. Opposed to the Quaker's execution, Cromwell interceded on Naylor's behalf and reminded Parliament that it was not a judicial body and had no right to try anyone.

uncovered. An ex-soldier and radical Leveller, Miles Sindercombe, had concocted a scheme to set fire to a chapel where Cromwell frequently prayed. In the confusion that would ensue, Sindercombe planned to shoot the Protector.

News of this conspiracy caused a great deal of alarm in Parliament. The members might disagree with some of the Protector's policies, but they recognized his contribution to the country's stability. In a congratulatory address to celebrate his escape, an offer was made: "that his Highness would be pleased to take upon him the government according to ancient constitution." In other words, in order for the country to have lasting security, Cromwell should become king.

This was not the first time such a suggestion had been made. However, now the offer took on new importance as large numbers of influential persons supported it. A few weeks later, in February 1657, a member of Parliament presented a motion to make Oliver Cromwell king, and to allow him to appoint his successor. By now it was obvious that a majority in Parliament supported this measure.

A big obstacle stood in the way — the army. So great was its opposition to Cromwell's becoming king that one officer, Thomas Pride, is said to have threatened to shoot him in the head the minute

Cromwell accepted the offer. On February 27 over 100 officers, including the major generals, met with Cromwell to demonstrate their hostility to the proposal. Cromwell responded by denying that he had anything to do with Parliament's motion to make him king. He did, however, observe that since there was a desperate need to dispense with arbitrary rule, some final settlement had to be found at once. Despite the persuasiveness of some of the Protector's arguments, the army continued to resist the creation of a monarchy.

Nevertheless, Parliament proceeded with the debate on a new constitution, to be known as "the Humble Petition and Advice." By March 1657 a stipulation to create a new House of Lords to balance and check the single House of Commons passed unanimously. Then on March 25, after a heated discussion, Parliament passed, by a vote of 123 to 62, a motion asking the Protector to accept the office and title of king.

When the parliamentary committee personally presented the petition to Cromwell, he expressed his great pleasure. "I am hugely taken with the thing," he said, "I think he is not worthy to live in England that is not." But as was his pattern, the Protector asked that he might have "some short time to ask counsel of God and of my own heart." On a matter of such importance, Cromwell would have to search his soul before reaching a decision.

He was a practical mystic, the most formidable and terrible of all combinations, uniting an inspiration derived from the celestial and supernatural with the energy of a mighty man of action; a great captain, but off the field seeming, like a thunderbolt, the agent of greater forces than himself; no hypocrite, but a defender of the faith; the raiser and maintainer of the Empire of England.
—LORD ROSEBERY

A grief-stricken Cromwell sits at the bedside of his daughter Elizabeth in August 1658, shortly before she died of cancer. Cromwell was shattered by Elizabeth's death and would die the following month.

Cromwell's death mask. The Lord Protector died on September 3, 1658, of natural causes. The fact that Cromwell passed away shortly after one of the greatest storms in living memory was regarded by many of his contemporaries as symbolic of the troubled times.

Most foreign observers residing in London were sure that Cromwell would accept the kingship. After all, that position seemed a fitting office for a man's ambition. For five weeks he held meetings with different groups, all urging him to hasten his choice. Lawyers assured him that his acceptance was the only way to establish a truly constitutional settlement. Cromwell wavered, appearing to lean toward this position. Yet just when it seemed that he would assume the throne, leading generals in the army threatened to resign. Their pressure proved sufficient to alter his decision.

Finally, on May 8, 1657, Cromwell returned an answer. "I cannot," he said, "undertake this government with the title of King." Thus, once more on a matter of great principle Cromwell decided to join with those in the army, whose ultimate support he regarded to be essential. Some two weeks later, when a new version of the "Petition and Advice" was presented to him, with the title of Protector replacing that of king, Cromwell gave his approval.

In Westminster Abbey on June 26 Cromwell was again installed as Lord Protector. On this occasion, however, the ceremony took on the grandeur of a royal coronation. The speaker, as the representative of Parliament, invested him in a robe of purple velvet, lined with ermine. A golden scepter was placed in his hands, just as in the days of royalty. Cromwell took his oath to maintain the Protestant religion and to preserve the peace and the rights of the three nations, England, Scotland, and Ireland. The trumpets rang out and the people shouted, "God save the Lord Protector." Oliver Cromwell had become king in all but name.

In many ways Cromwell's powers under the "Petition and Advice" were more extensive than ever before. For the first time he possessed the authority to name his own successor. Moreover, he could personally choose the members of the restored House of Lords. Also, the previous Parliament had granted his government a generous amount of money to cover all expenditures, including the additional revenues needed to finance the current naval war with Spain. As a result, the Cromwellian Protectorate seemed to be stronger and more secure than ever.

When the new Parliament met in January 1658, the Protector greeted the delegates with confidence and praise. In his opening speech he told them that they would be "the repairers of breaches, and the restorers of paths to dwell in," and "shall be called the blessed of the Lord." Once again, however, Cromwell had let his natural optimism get the better of him. The reality turned out to be much harsher.

By selecting allies to be members of the House of Lords, Cromwell removed many of his supporters from the House of Commons. Leading republicans, many of whom had been excluded from the previous Parliaments, had returned in force. Their hostility toward the army, and toward all efforts to diminish parliamentary supremacy, was as strong as ever. Like-minded members banded together, losing few opportunities to oppose governmental policies. This opposition party proved quite obstructive. They questioned the need for another house of Parliament, and many even refused to acknowledge the legitimacy of the new government on the grounds that they had not approved its creation.

Four days after he opened Parliament, Cromwell delivered a second speech. He warned of the serious dangers facing the country from foreign enemies and from allies of Charles II. But the republicans, who now controlled the Commons, would not bend. They disliked the new government, finding it remarkably similar to the old Stuart monarchy. "To betray the liberties of the people of England," one of them answered, "that I cannot." With parliamentary business grinding to a standstill little could be accomplished. Some of the republicans drew up a petition, which got 10,000 signatures in London, to demand limitations on the Protector's power over the military.

To Cromwell the problem with this Parliament seemed depressingly familiar. On February 4, 1658, he summoned both Houses together for the purpose of dismissing them. In a brief speech he described his reluctance to exercise his extreme power in such a negative fashion. "There is not a man living can say I sought it, no, not a man nor a woman treading

Cromwell's son Richard (1626–1712), who became Lord Protector upon his father's death, proved an ineffectual ruler and was dismissed from office by Parliament in 1659. He then retired from political life completely.

upon English ground. . . . The nation is in likelihood of running into more confusion in these 15 or 16 days that you have sat, than it hath been from the rising of the last session to this day." Having no other recourse, Cromwell put an end to their sessions. "Let God be judge between you and me," he concluded.

This speech ended Cromwell's last Parliament. Whether he would have summoned another one is hard to determine. Knowing his relentlessly optimistic nature, he would have most likely tried to come up with the successful formula that had managed to elude him so far. But running Parliament effectively, the way Queen Elizabeth had managed to do almost a century earlier, was not one of his strengths. To his credit, unlike most modern dictators, Cromwell resisted the temptation to rule the country on his own. He continued to seek a work-

Returning to England at Parliament's invitation, Charles II lands at Dover on May 25, 1660. Charles's desire to avenge his father's death was fulfilled on January 30, 1661, when the bodies of Cromwell, Henry Ireton, and John Bradshaw (1602–59) — the presiding judge at Charles I's trial — were removed from their coffins, hanged, and then beheaded.

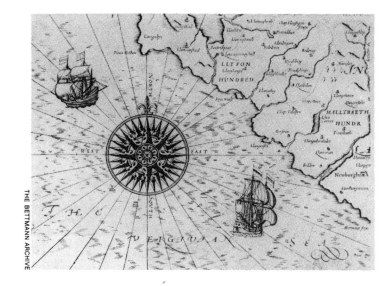

A section from a 1676 map entitled "Empire of Great Britain."

able government that included an important voice for the nation, through representatives in Parliament. But, given his reliance upon the army, necessitated in part by an unstable and dangerous situation, Cromwell would never agree to hand total authority over to the Parliament.

With England's powerful navy dominating a declining Spanish Empire, and with all royalist and religious threats to Cromwell's rule under control, the Protectorate in 1658 appeared to be in a relatively strong position. Finance, however, continued to cause difficulties. Supporting a sizable standing army had put the government in debt, and this situation could only be erased with help from a Parliament that no longer met. Moreover, the structure of England depended upon Cromwell the individual, and unfortunately he had begun to age considerably. The strains of his life showed on his face.

Now 59 years of age, the weight of his many responsibilities and disappointments led to a marked physical decline. During the first half of the year he was frequently ill. His failure to work out an agreement with this last Parliament particularly disheartened him. Like many famous leaders, both before and after, he began to regret the burdens of office, wondering out loud if he would have been

Charles II's decision to proceed against those responsible for his father's execution was considered unnecessarily divisive by many of the Puritans.

better off had he remained a country farmer. "I would have lived under my woodside, to have kept a flock of sheep, rather than undertook such a government as this is." But for Cromwell, his sense of duty did not permit the luxury of a peaceful life.

Compounding his growing despondency was the sorrow he felt for the loss of loved ones. A son-in-law died in February 1658 and in August, after a long illness, his favorite daughter, Elizabeth, died. He never really recovered emotionally from Elizabeth's death.

Soon after Elizabeth's funeral Cromwell came down with a fever. At first he appeared to recover, but then had a relapse. Spending his last days in reflection and prayer, he is said to have prayed not for himself, since he was confident of his fate, but for his people. He hoped that they might still unite in a common cause. Some time before the end, the Protector named his eldest son, Richard Cromwell, to be his successor.

At 4 A.M. on September 3, 1658, Oliver Cromwell died. It was the anniversary of his lucky day: the day when he had won his spectacular battles at Dunbar and Worcester.

Not being able to work out a permanent political settlement had frustrated Cromwell. Given his political views and the existing situation in England, it is doubtful that he could have ever succeeded.

His son, Richard, had little other than his last name to enable him to bring about the solution which had eluded Oliver. Over the army, the main source of his father's power, Richard had little influence. As a result, he exercised even less control over Parliament, for he had no leverage with which to negotiate with the politicians. Nor did he possess the prestige derived from Oliver's stature as a military leader. During Richard's short 20-month rule, the army and Parliament became once more divided. Furthermore, the army split into various factions, thereby losing its effectiveness as a force to order the country when Parliament had to be dismissed.

Soon after, Richard stepped down and Charles II was restored to the throne. At the end of April 1660 a free Parliament met, and a month later King

Charles II reentered London in triumph. The Stuart monarchy once again ruled England.

After punishing the surviving "Regicides," those responsible for his father's execution, Charles II demanded vengeance on the dead. In January 1661 the coffins of Oliver Cromwell and Henry Ireton were taken from their graves. On the morning of January 30, the 12th anniversary of Charles I's execution, their bodies, along with that of the deceased presiding judge, John Bradshaw, were removed from their coffins. Then these three, side by side in death, were hanged from a tree. At the day's end they were taken down, their heads cut off and then placed on poles for display.

The desecration of his memory, the revenge of the living on the dead, was an attempt to tarnish Cromwell's reputation. For more than two centuries historians and politicians saw him in a negative light. Viewed as a usurper mainly by conservatives, he was condemned as an ambitious man who violated his country's supposedly peaceful traditions. A more favorable view of Cromwell emerged in the last century, as people began to recognize that he had supported certain humane goals. Like the liberal-minded of the 19th century, Cromwell favored religious toleration and, in theory at least, the supremacy of Parliament. He could thus be placed among those who favored England's development of democratic government. And as England became the strongest power on earth, Cromwell's early contribution to this world role could no longer be denied. Nor could military scholars ignore his superior ability as a general. His talents in this area rank him with the most famous soldiers in all of history.

Today historians view Cromwell within the complexities of his own time and place. More stress is placed on the social, economic, and even religious aspects of 17th-century England, and Cromwell is now seen as reflecting the various tensions of his own society. Whatever the interpretation, it is now fully recognized that he was one of the greatest of all Englishmen. England's traditions and heritage cannot be fully appreciated without acknowledging Cromwell's significant contributions.

Cromwell as portrayed by Dutch painter Rembrandt van Rijn (1606–69). Many of those who had criticized Cromwell during his lifetime began to modify their assessments as it became apparent that Charles II's reign would be undistinguished at best. In 1667 Secretary of the Admiralty Samuel Pepys (1633–1703), wrote: "Everybody do now-a-days reflect upon Oliver and commend him, what brave things he did and made all the neighbour princes fear him."

Further Reading

Ashley, Maurice. *The Greatness of Oliver Cromwell*. New York: Macmillan Publishing Company, 1958.

Buchan, John. *Oliver Cromwell*. London: Richard Clay & Co., Ltd., 1972.

Cromwell, Oliver. *Letters and Speeches*. New York: George Routledge & Sons, Ltd., 1932.

Fraser, Antonia. *Cromwell: The Lord Protector*. New York: Alfred A. Knopf, Inc., 1973.

Hill, Christopher. *The Century of Revolution*. New York: Oxford University Press, 1971.

———. *God's Englishman: Oliver Cromwell and the English Revolution*. New York: The Dial Press, 1970.

———. *Intellectual Origins of the English Revolution*. New York: Oxford University Press, 1965.

Roots, Ivan, ed. *Cromwell: A Profile*. New York: Farrar, Straus & Giroux, Inc., 1973.

Chronology

April 25, 1599	Born Oliver Cromwell in Huntingdon, England
1616–17	Attends Cambridge University
June 24, 1617	Robert Cromwell, Oliver's father, dies
Aug. 22, 1620	Cromwell marries Elizabeth Bourchier
1625	Charles I succeeds James I as king of England
June 1628	Cromwell attends first Parliament as representative to the House of Commons from Huntingdon
1628	Parliament enacts the Petition of Right, prohibiting the king from imposing taxes without Parliament's consent
1629–40	Charles I dissolves Parliament, levies severe taxes, and persecutes Puritans during period called "The Eleven Years of Tyranny"
April 1640	Charles I opens Parliament and then three weeks later closes it (the Short Parliament)
Nov. 1640	The Long Parliament begins
Aug. 1642	First Civil War begins Cromwell raises his own army to fight for Parliament against Charles I
Jan. 1644	Made lieutenant general
July 2, 1644	Leads Parliament to victory at the Battle of Marston Moor
April 3, 1645	Self-Denying Ordinance passed, requiring all members of Parliament to resign their army posts
June 20, 1646	First Civil War ends as Charles I surrenders at Oxford
Oct. 1647	Officers and Agitators in Cromwell's army conduct debate over a new British constitution (the Putney Debate)
Feb. 1648	Second Civil War begins
Aug. 1648	Royalist army suffers complete defeat at the Battle of Preston
Dec. 6, 1648	Colonel Thomas Pride eliminates members of Parliament thought to be sympathetic to the king (Pride's Purge)
Jan. 1649	Charles I is tried and executed in London
May 1649	House of Commons establishes the English Commonwealth
Aug. 1649	Cromwell begins campaign to "pacify" the Irish
1650	England fights war with Scotland
April 19, 1653	Cromwell terminates the Rump Parliament
Dec. 16, 1653	A new government, called the Protectorate, is formed after the dissolution of the Barebones Parliament Cromwell is installed as Lord Protector
Sept. 3, 1654	First Protectorate Parliament is convened
1655	Cromwell imposes military rule after closing the first Protectorate Parliament
Sept. 3, 1658	Dies, aged 59, and is buried at Westminster Abbey

Index

Lawrence Kaplan is currently Professor of History at
the City College of the City University of New York. He
holds a B.A. from Queens College, an M.A. from Brown
University, and a Ph.D. from Washington University
in St. Louis, Missouri. Professor Kaplan is the author
of various articles and reviews on English history, and
the book, *Politics and Religion during the English
Revolution*. He is married and is the father of two
daughters.

Arthur M. Schlesinger, jr., taught history at Harvard
for many years and is currently Albert Schweitzer Professor of the Humanities at City University of New
York. He is the author of numerous highly praised
works in American history and has twice been
awarded the Pulitzer Prize. He served in the White
House as special assistant to Presidents Kennedy and
Johnson.